Mia Iwama Hastings *as told to her by* Mimi Iwama

The HEIGHT

of

FEARLESSNESS

A True Story of the Power of Perspective

RIVER GROVE
BOOKS

This book is based on true events from Mimi Iwama's early life and reflects some of her present recollections of experiences over time as told to the author. The story, words, and portayal of events are the author's alone. Some names, facts, characters, and other details have been changed by the author for creative purposes and to protect the privacy of others. Some events have been compressed, and all dialogue and scenes have been recreated by the author.

Published by River Grove Books
Austin, TX
www.rivergrovebooks.com

Distributed by River Grove Books

Design and composition by Greenleaf Book Group
Cover design by Greenleaf Book Group
Cover images used under license from ©Shutterstock.com/Evgeniya Mokkeva; ©Shutterstock.com/Amanita Silvicora

Publisher's Cataloging-in-Publication data is available.

Print ISBN: 978-1-63299-257-4

eBook ISBN: 978-1-63299-258-1

First Edition

For Masuko to honor her wisdom, love and courage and to share her extraordinary lessons with the world; and for Frank, who encouraged us to tell this story.

CHAPTER 1

KANSHA / APPRECIATION

Freedom from fear gives you wings to soar. My mother's words echo in my mind and are etched on my heart. This is the story of how I conquered fear.

My destiny was shaped by mystic forces thousands of years ago when the islands of Japan were created by the Shinto gods. These immortal beings gave spirits to the mountains, trees, rocks, and waterfalls. A sacred essence, or *kami*, flows through all creatures, objects, and elements of nature like a vast and undulating river, connecting all life with a deep and eternal spirit. On the southern island of Kyushu in Kumamoto city (named "Higo" prior to the Meiji Restoration), there is a remarkable little hill called "Hanaokayama," meaning "little flower mountain." It grew gradually over time, rising above the tranquil city like a mysterious guardian in the mist. It is covered with cherry trees, which bloom magnificently every spring and give the mountain its name.

Hanaokayama has been my meditation hall, my refuge, and my inspiration. It was here, seventy-two years ago, that my mother taught me about love and fearlessness and gave me an invisible weapon like the sword of my samurai ancestors.

I journeyed along that winding path until I reached the mountain's peak and felt like I was soaring above the city like a hawk. The active volcano Mount Aso looms far beyond, immortalized in Japanese mythology—at once exhilarating and terrifying with its fiery secret. The crowning glory of Hanaokayama is a grand Buddhist temple. Alongside this is a magnificent red Shinto *torii*, or shrine gate, formed of two pillars and two perfectly balanced lintels. It is a gateway to a mystical world that has transformed my life.

Now that I am eighty-one, I understand my mother's courage and her stoic acceptance of the impermanence of life. Certainty is a mere illusion; we live in a constant state of flux. The war had taken everything from us, and she knew her strength was fading day by day. All she had left to give me was her wisdom about survival: her knowledge on overcoming life's challenges. Her lessons have empowered me to be fearless and to triumph over suffering and despair. Now I would like to share her wisdom and legacy with the world to honor her memory and courage.

From this remarkable vantage point at the top of Hanaokayama, you can feel the city's deeply rooted history—as ancient as the trees on the mountain. Kumamoto has a renowned castle and a proud tradition of samurai warriors, including my own ancestors and the most famous warrior of all: the legendary master swordsman Miyamoto Musashi. My mother told me how he perfected the art of fighting with two swords and how, undefeated in battle, he hid in a cave among the hills near Kumamoto to write *Go Rin No Sho: The Book of Five Rings*, a guide to battle strategy. In this book, he reveals that his strength of mind is the key to his mastery of the sword. According to legend, in 1645 he was buried upright in a full suit of armor in Musashizuka Park in Kumamoto near the old road to Edo (now Tokyo), so he could keep watch over Lord Hosokawa's procession to visit the shogun. I have seen his simple, dark gravestone sheltered by verdant trees in the tranquil park. I often wonder if his spirit still keeps watch over travelers on the road.

As I child, I heard the eternal, ghostly echoes of Musashi's steel blades clashing against his rivals' swords in the mountain. His strength of mind and body seems to flow in this mystical place. The flawless swords he bore were produced in the timeless, traditional way: hammered repeatedly in the searing heat until they glistened silver and achieved the perfect sharpness for victory in battle. My mother would remind me of this. Like the steel of the sword, my character would be shaped and refined by life's challenges. I would emerge even stronger in the face of adversity, glittering and triumphant.

Hanaokayama has many faces and moods. She wears the colors of the season, which change and transform with the rising sun and silvery moon. She is at once ephemeral in her transitory beauty and immutable in her solidity. She is mysterious and majestic, serene and silent. The wisdom of ages rests here and flows through this sacred place.

At the beginning of each spring, her green face gradually transforms into a little flower mountain, covered with silken cherry blossom petals like snow. My mother said that the cherry blossom was a symbol of the samurai warrior: resilient, courageous, and fearless in the face of death. When the blossoms fall to the ground in battle, they fade away in an act of noble sacrifice. They are a reminder of our own frailty and mortality, the beauty of the fleeting moment and the connection between heaven and earth. While we admire these perfect and glorious flowers, we know that they will soon fall to the ground, decorating the earth and becoming part of the soil that helps new blossoms grow.

I remember exactly how my mother looked the day we first arrived at the mountain. Her dark hair was pinned into a tidy bun. She was very petite and thin and had the gentle and controlled demeanor of a refined lady from Nagasaki. She managed to look elegant wearing a simple *monpei*, comprised of a short-sleeved dark cotton blouse and trousers. This was the typical attire of country farmers, yet her grace elevated its stark simplicity.

I wore a miniature version of my mother's monpei. My skin was golden like the sun.

My mother smiled gently and spoke softly as we walked. "Mi-chan," she said, "I have received permission for us to live here for a while. There is a small house where we can stay until you are feeling better. You must rest in solitude, and you will grow strong again with nature as your guide and comfort. The mountain's air has healing powers."

My mother's dark eyes looked thoughtful and expectant behind her gold-framed glasses. I was so excited to see our new house after everything we had suffered. My memories of the war were so vivid in my mind. The screams of terror and blaring air raid sirens still haunted my dreams and left me shaking in fear.

Now it seemed as though we had entered a mystical land, enchanted and protected from danger and decay. The blossoms' sweet scent filled my nostrils.

"Spring is here and with it new life and a fresh beginning," she said. "The mountain is already turning white with cherry blossoms. Our new house is surrounded by ancient, towering trees with deep roots in this rich soil blessed by kami. You already have tree friends.

Ureshi desho, you must be happy, Mi-chan. Soon you will discover how lovely this place is."

"It's amazing," I observed. "I can't believe it's so quiet. I can only hear the sounds of birds, and the wind in the leaves."

"It is Hanaokayama's song," my mother replied. "It echoes through the mountain."

I stopped to listen. There was a faint noise in the background. First I thought it was the buzzing of insects. Then I realized it was distant, rhythmic chanting.

"Oka-chan," I called, curious. "Do you hear that? What's that?"

"They are young Buddhist monks," my mother explained. "They believe the chanting helps them receive wisdom and focus their minds to save us all from suffering."

The sound was strangely soothing to hear, as though the mountain were humming. It blended into the hills with the birdsong until the two seemed to harmonize.

I noticed the same sounds in succession. "Are they repeating the same words?" I asked

"That's right, Mi-chan," she replied. "They repeat the same prayers to help them focus on what they are saying. The more they say it, the more they understand. They repeat their prayers together until they speak as one. Their words blend together into a single sound with all of nature, until they are one with the birds and the wind in the trees."

The winding path was beginning to get a bit steeper as we walked, and I noticed my mother's pace had slowed considerably.

"Oka-chan, are you tired, are you all right?" I asked worriedly. "We can stop and sit for a while." I felt guilty that I had rushed her in my eagerness to see the house.

"Thank you, Mi-chan, but please don't worry. I'm so pleased that you like it here," she replied. "This has always been my favorite place in Kumamoto."

"I love it," I said. "There are so many colors. It looks like everything has been painted!" Everywhere I looked there was life, and it seemed to center around this mountain, as though its very essence was the source of everything.

We had arrived at the top of the mountain above a large open space overlooking the serene hills. I was astonished by the dramatic view of the city of Kumamoto that lay before me, bathed in mellow, shimmering sunlight like liquid gold. The city had suffered immense devastation during the war, but from here the scene looked picturesque and tranquil. Hanaokayama had an eternally peaceful feeling, surrounded by the majesty of nature and seemingly separate from the destruction in the valley below.

This place was steeped in the city's ancient history, and its deeply rooted mythology seemed woven into the very fabric of these hills. Our magical mountain was enveloped in flower petals and ribbons of light. I thought of the mystical lands in the folk stories my mother told me, full of glowing red skies and lilac mountains inhabited by mighty dragons and mischievous monkeys. I felt there was a deeper presence, a living spirit, in this mountain.

"What an incredible view! Is this where we're going to live?" I asked excitedly. I couldn't believe it. It was like a dream.

"Yes," she replied. "I knew you would like it."

I caught sight of a small wooden house with paper *shoji* screens. It had a little forest of its own protecting it, and I knew instinctively that this must be our house. It matched my mother's description exactly. Beside it you could see the majestic view of the entire city. To the right there was a slightly larger house with a dark wood *engawa*, or veranda.

"Oka-chan, look at how enormous these trees are!" I said and ran enthusiastically to show her the trees, which formed a ring around the house like gigantic guards encircling us.

"They must be so strong with deep roots in the soil. I'm going to greet them."

I bowed before the tallest tree and said, "*Konnichiwa*, hello. My name is Mimi. Everyone calls me Mi-chan." I saw the tree sway a little, and I knew this was a sign.

"My mother and I are going to live here until I get strong. Please protect us. *Domo arigato gozaimasu*, thank you," I said and bowed very low to show my respect. I knew the tree must be very old and had seen many adventures on this mountain.

Suddenly, I felt a breeze. I heard the gentle rustling of tree branches. One of the branches almost touched me as it moved.

"Oka-chan," I shouted with my excitement, "The trees are going to protect us. Aren't we lucky to have such friends?"

My mother smiled gently and replied, "You are such a free spirit, Mi-chan. You make friends with everyone, and you respect all living things. You can speak to the trees and the hills."

"I love this place, Oka-chan," I said. "I'm going to go look at the house. I can't wait to see what the rooms are like!"

I ran to the house eagerly and slid back the shoji screen to see what surprises awaited us. It was made of polished wood and translucent white rice paper and glided smoothly across the floor like a leaf on a stream.

"Oka-chan, look at this!" I exclaimed as I surveyed the clean, bright room bathed in light. Its simplicity was stunning. The shoji screen cast dancing squares of light on the *tatami*. I was enveloped by a soothing sense of calm.

"This room is a meditation room for tired travelers, so they can rest and clear their minds. What a beautiful tatami!" she exclaimed as she touched the smooth, clean woven mat which covered the floor. It was immaculate.

I took off my shoes and put them down neatly side by side to show my mother that I was a lady like her. I had missed the familiar feel of the woven straw tatami on my bare feet. Simple things we took for granted before the war were now indescribably precious. They were remnants of the tradition and stability we once knew before our lives were torn apart by chaos.

"I am so glad you like this room," my mother said. "Your brother said he would help bring a few of your things later to save us having to carry them up the mountain." We had lost practically everything during the war. All of my belongings fit into one worn bag. This included a small doll my mother had made for me during the war. It was my prized possession.

"Isn't this a lovely house?" she asked. "Do you like it?"

"It's a perfect house! Oka-chan, *arigato*, thank you for bringing me here," I replied. "We are so lucky to be able to stay here."

As I turned, I saw a stately looking man standing outside by the door. I nearly jumped when I saw him. It was as though he had appeared by magic from thin air.

"*Konnichiwa*, hello. *Do desuka, mani ai masuka*? How is it? Is this adequate for you?" he asked. He was an elderly man wearing a long white kimono with a shorter black robe over it. He had a long white sash, and on his feet he wore white *tabi* socks with *zori*, special slippers. He was dignified and imposing-looking, yet his eyes were kind and made me feel at ease. His voice was calm and deep. The subtle wrinkles on his face were like grooves in the bark of a venerable tree. He must be the priest who had helped my mother gain permission for us to live here.

"*Honto ni arigato gozaimasu.* Thank you so much," my mother replied as she bowed deeply to the monk for a long time. I copied her.

"Hello, Mi-chan," he spoke to me. His aura instantly made me feel more peaceful. "How old are you? You seem to be very clever."

"*Arigato gozaimasu*, thank you. I am nine years old."

"You are wise for your age," he replied. "Please obey and help your mother and get well soon."

"*Hai*, yes." I bowed very deep as my mother had taught me to show respect to my elders.

The priest patted my head and smiled.

"My family is so grateful for your kindness. I will never forget your generosity. *Arigato gozaimasu*, thank you," I said, bowing again.

"You two must be tired after your long travels. You should rest," he said.

"We are weary, but we enjoyed the walk," my mother replied.

"Are you thirsty? Let me show you where the well is. We have fresh water, but it is hidden," he explained. "I can show you. I can also point out the steps near the side of the house. This is the easiest way to walk to the town."

"Thank you." My mother bowed again. "If it isn't too much trouble, we would be grateful for your help."

"It is no trouble at all," he replied with a kind smile. "The water from the well is refreshing and pure. It's from a natural spring. Soon you will know this mountain as well as I do, but for now, I shall be your guide. She is full of surprises, and there are always new paths to explore."

We followed him. He walked with his slow, stately pace beside stacked gray stones with tall wildflowers and vines growing all over them. Everything surrounding us was so green and rich in color, reminding me of the brush strokes of my mother's vibrant watercolor paintings. I was amazed by how vivid the vines and grass appeared in the sunlight, like sparkling emeralds catching the light, creating multiplying pools of verdant color. After climbing down a short flight of stone steps, I saw a small well made out of worn clay, covered in fresh moss dotted with flecks of water that shimmered in the sunlight. There was a wooden bucket loosely tied to the side of the well with a coarse rope. Beside this was a long gray stone that formed a natural bench for weary travelers. It had been worn smooth over time. I wondered how many people had sat there over hundreds of years as they came to this sacred place to find freedom from suffering.

"You simply take the bucket and lower it into the well until it fills with water," the priest explained. "Then you pull it back up with the rope carefully so as not to spill it. The water is like milk. It comes out very thin and pale but is very easy to pour and safe to drink. Mi-chan, please bring the ladle here so you and your mother can taste the water."

"*Hai*, yes," I replied. I picked up the wooden ladle resting in the corner by the well.

"Thank you, Mi-chan. I'll let you try it," the priest said. "Take your time. You have everything you need in the house. Please just relax and rest."

My mother bowed low.

"Mi-chan, look after your mother, and take care of yourself," he said. "Hanaokayama is the perfect place for walking meditation. Walk and observe the glorious nature around you. Empty yourself of your thoughts and worries, and let the peace of this place fill your spirit."

"*Arigato gozaimasu*, thank you," we said and bowed.

"Thank you for helping your mother," he said to me, smiling. "Enjoy the rest of the day, and follow the path where it leads. Let Hanaokayama guide you on your journey. As the poet Basho said, we shouldn't follow the footsteps of the wise. Instead, we should seek the wisdom they sought. You will find what they sought here if you open your mind to the possibilities of this place."

We bowed again and watched the priest until he disappeared up the hill and vanished as mysteriously as he had appeared.

I looked at the well. The water was curious. It had such a strange chalky color. *This water must be milk*, I thought. *This mountain must be enchanted.* I wanted to taste it.

"Oka-chan, please sit down. I will give you some magical water," I said.

She laughed, "The priest said that this is special water, protected by all the flowers and plants of the mountain."

I grabbed the bucket and dropped it in the well, like the priest had told us. Some chalky water flowed into the bucket. I lifted the bucket out very slowly, but triumphantly.

"Oka-chan, please try some milk-water," I said. The little wooden ladle was perfectly made, and poured neatly. I handed it to my mother. She took a sip and then I did.

The priest was right. The well water tasted smooth. I felt it cleansed my mind and body. It tasted of purity and smelled deeply of nature.

Once we were back at the house, my mother explained that tonight was going to be a night of celebration to honor our ancestors. We would be enjoying a special dinner called *shojin ryori*, which is traditional vegetarian food that Buddhist monks eat.

That night, my mother thanked our ancestors and departed friends for protecting our lives. She said that my life was the greatest gift she had ever received.

Even though the food was plain and the portion was small, dinner seemed like a joyous celebration. I especially enjoyed the soup with seaweed in its clear broth. The priest had given us green tea, and its delicate aroma lifted my spirits.

My mother told me about the history of this place and how ancient the little mountain was. I loved hearing her exciting stories about Kumamoto's history, the castle, and the elegant ladies and courageous lords who had lived here.

"The mountain changes with the seasons," she explained to me. "This is my favorite season, when she is covered with cherry blossoms, wildflowers, and leafy trees that dance in the breeze. In the summer, she wears vivid green grass illuminated by sunlight. During the autumn, she begins to grow pale and subdued, and in winter she is dark like the sky and the trees are bare. The full moon shines very brightly then, when it turns cold at night."

"I'm so happy that spring is here," I said. "Everything is alive!"

"Yes," my mother agreed. "We should sing a song to celebrate."

"Sakura!" I said. "The cherry blossoms are here!" "Sakura" was my mother's favorite song and she often sang it to me, especially when I was scared during the war.

My mother's voice was as clear as a bell. After we finished singing, she said, "I am so glad you enjoy music as much as I do. Remember Mi-chan—we should always have sunshine in our hearts and a song on our lips, and we shall never be unhappy. Music can transport you anywhere and lift your spirits."

"*Hai*, yes," I nodded.

"Mi-chan, that reminds me," my mother said. "I have a special gift for you."

She took out a notebook that she had fashioned for me. It was made of card stock and half the size of a newspaper, cut into two pieces and sewn together with several sheets of rice paper in between. She had embellished it with painted cherry blossoms, and on its cover she had painted in exquisite calligraphy "Mimi *no Michi*," meaning "Mimi's Roadmap." The book was small and dainty. My mother never used a pencil or pen to write. She was an expert brush painter, and she could control every brush stroke with precision.

"I made this for you," she explained. "The size will suit you perfectly since you're small. This is for your lessons, which we'll start tomorrow. I have so much to teach you."

"Thank you so much, Oka-chan," I replied. "It's beautiful, and I shall treasure it."

"You're a very kind girl, Mi-chan," she said. "Whatever happens in our lives, we should always have *kansha*, appreciation, in our hearts and remember that we are part of nature and live in harmony with the universe. We are all connected by invisible threads."

My mother used the word "kansha" so often. It is a Japanese word that means something deeper than appreciation. Its meaning is rooted in the Buddhist recognition that everything that happens is connected, and there is a reason behind every occurrence. She taught me that we must see and appreciate this interconnectedness and treat all people and nature with love and respect.

After dinner, my mother and I looked at the spring moon and the glimmering stars in the indigo sky. We watched the gently fluttering silhouettes of the tall trees that encircled the house. It was so still in the evening that I couldn't hear anything at all except the occasional rustling of leaves in the gentle breeze.

"I like it here, Oka-chan," I declared.

"I'm so glad, Mi-chan," she replied. There was silence as we watched the stars. After a while my mother spoke again: "Do you see that very bright star, Mi-chan? That is a planet."

"That's amazing," I said. "Do you think Musashi-sensei saw it when *he* lived here?"

My mother smiled. "Perhaps he did. This very same light may have guided his path at night."

I thought of the great samurai warrior walking on this flower mountain at night with his stealthy, silent footsteps. He might have stepped in the very same spot where we now stood. The thought was inspiring and made me appreciate how special this place was—and how tiny I was in comparison to its storied history, like a single black dot of ink on an infinite white scroll of rice paper.

As we looked up at the night sky, suddenly there was a brilliant streak of light across the vast, dark canvas. I gasped and held my breath, watching it move across the sky in a trail of glowing stardust, only to disappear just as mysteriously.

"A shooting star!" I exclaimed.

"That's right, Mi-chan," my mother said. "Isn't it stunning?"

I nodded. "What is it made of?" I asked.

"Meteors are fragments of old comets or asteroids," she told me. "This must have been a piece of something very ancient: an asteroid that is thousands of years old."

I gazed upwards in amazement. This seemed like a magical sign.

That night, I slept on a soft, clean futon. I thought how lucky I was to have a family, and to be safe at last in such an enchanted, tranquil place surrounded by the spirit of nature and the glimmer of ancient stars.

Show *kansha*, appreciation and gratitude,
for all positive aspects of your life.

二

CHAPTER 2

SAKURA / BLOSSOM

I was only three years old when Japan attacked Pearl Harbor in 1941, starting the war that would change our lives and country forever. By the time the war ended in 1945, I was seven. I have very little memory of the war's beginning and recall only fragments of conversation about Pearl Harbor, the strains of war songs, and an overwhelming atmosphere of fear and uncertainty that pervaded our lives like a deep fog. I remember seeing families bidding tearful goodbyes at the train station as they sent their young children away to the countryside for their safety. Our childhoods were taken from us, collectively, and our lives would never be the same.

From January 1944 until August 1945, the US targeted more than sixty Japanese cities and dropped 157,000 tons of conventional bombs on military targets—many of them in areas densely populated by civilians. Nearly one-third of Kumamoto was destroyed during the war. The air was constantly full of smoke and the melody of nationalistic songs, reminding us that we were all suffering to serve our emperor.

The devastating attacks on my city by American B-29 bombers are etched in my memory. I remember the daily struggle for survival amid the horrors of the war: the endless screams and sirens that pierced the sky, the crackling sound of fire as it destroyed homes, and piles of lifeless bodies soaked in blood. I can still feel our helplessness as we scurried like mice exhausted from evading the predators circling above us in the sky and the sea of flames that threatened to engulf us. We had to keep living and hoping our lives would be spared, even when we saw death and devastation everywhere. The American military began to realize that the Japanese would not surrender, and so they kept increasing the scale of their attacks.

The 37th infantry division of the Imperial Japanese Army was established in Kumamoto in 1939 to protect the civilians. I was only one year old at the time, but this news meant that the peace of our lives would be shattered. Even children were not allowed their innocence. My brother had to go to the military base in Kumamoto to help with assembly line and clearing up duties. Boys and young men were taught to use rifles for killing and self-defense. Young women were taught to practice *naginata*, a form of self-defense performed with an ancient samurai weapon once used by my ancestors: a long pole with a spear at its end. Food supplies were hard to come by, and dried goods and rice were among the most precious commodities.

Many of the men in our city joined the fierce *kamikaze* pilots, accepting the inevitability of death with stoic determination fueled by their belief in the higher cause they were serving. They say that faith in something bigger than ourselves can overcome even our greatest fear. The kamikaze knew their inescapable fate was to perish in service of our emperor. They would attack military ships, their planes only equipped with enough fuel for the final descent into attack. There was no door on the pilot's side from which he could escape. The kamikaze were human torpedoes, suicide bombers. For them, this was the greatest and most honorable sacrifice they could make, a visible sign of their allegiance to our emperor.

According to Japanese law, the eldest son was spared from joining the kamikaze so he could maintain stability at home, while other sons were required to join the kamikaze. My mother was grateful that my brother's life had been spared.

In the morning, the air raid siren's piercing cry of warning struck terror into my heart and signaled another firebomb attack by the American planes. I jumped to my feet frantically. My thick hat felt heavy against my forehead and ears, yet it couldn't drown out that desperate wail. Dressed in a dark shirt and long trousers, I looked like a foot soldier from samurai times with my homemade helmet fashioned from two pieces of cloth sewn together and filled with heavy cotton. I wore slip-on shoes so we could run at a moment's notice.

Air raid shelters of all kinds of shapes were built across Kumamoto to protect us from the incessant attacks. We called these *bokugyo*, "little holes," to help conceal people during an air raid. Most were very crude open pit shelters dug by the residents of our city. Some had roofs made of bamboo poles, rafters, and soil, with plants positioned to help conceal those hiding inside.

As the planes approached, we would scatter like mice to the nearest shelters, caves, or holes. A cluster of planes, sometimes as many as twenty, would fly low to the ground, dropping firebombs to devastate the city. The sound was unbearable and sent chills down my spine.

At night, we covered our lamps with thick black cloths to conceal our houses from the planes. We were all in hiding. The soldiers installed searchlights on the ground to pierce the darkness of night and keep watch for any air attacks. We had no rest for days and nights on end, leaving us all feeling like zombies. The attacks were constant, and we always had to be prepared. I lived in constant fear of the sound of approaching planes. I even imagined the phantom sound of planes. I couldn't stop the chattering of my teeth and the constant shaking of my body. Every sound made me jump in anticipation. My scalp burned from lice, and my sore skin stung from the fleabites on my arms and legs. I was dirty and exhausted, and my stomach always felt the sharp pangs of hunger. Every time I closed my eyes, I could see houses burning. I heard people screaming and sirens wailing, warning us of another attack. I couldn't cry. Everyone else was crying for their lost loved ones. My mother and I were still alive, so we were the fortunate ones. Fear was all I felt, but everyone around me told me to have courage.

All I wanted was a quiet, safe place and sleep. I was so tired, but anxiety and adrenaline coursed through me constantly, making rest impossible. Even when I wasn't running myself, my thoughts ran circles in my head like a hamster on a wheel. I replayed the horrors I had seen over and over until I wanted to scream. I saw faces warped by the agony of pain and fright, and heard the screams as houses and bodies alike were consumed by flames. The sight of the flames engulfing them and the sickening smell of burning flesh were absolutely horrific. Sometimes at night, the sky would be illuminated in a ghastly blood red from the firebombs, and I thought demons had taken control of our city. Sparks would fall on buildings and people and burst into flames, leaving only burnt rubble and corpses in the morning light.

I only slept hour-by-hour in the night, like a half-awake bird ready to take flight at a moment's notice. Sometimes I slept in the shelter at night, despite the discomfort. It was so hot and humid. We were packed inside like sticky, dirty passengers on a boat trying desperately to escape. None of us could bathe. We were lucky to have a sponge to wash off with now and again, but even this was a rare luxury during the war, when supplies were scarce and we were constantly moving or hiding.

I saw hundreds of innocent children and elderly women suffering in silence, demonstrating extraordinary courage and compassion in their daily struggle for survival. As my mother said about samurai swords, we did not know how strong we really were until we were tested by flames. When I heard babies crying, I felt their sorrow and helplessness deep in my soul. We were all as powerless as they were. We had not chosen this fate—it had been thrust upon us. Every day, our food portions would grow smaller and smaller, but we shared what little we had with others. Our deeply ingrained sense of community spirit and loyalty did not abandon us, even when we were faced with abject survival. I was grateful that my mother was always by my side, and when I saw so many children who had lost their parents, I reminded myself how fortunate I was.

That morning, I was accompanying my mother to find her friend and ensure she was safe. As we walked along the road, the siren's wail began again, signaling another attack.

"We must go, Mi-chan," my mother whispered. "Quickly, run to the shelter."

Clouds of dust, ash, and smoke rose above Kumamoto as we ran. The morning was so cloudy, hot, and muggy that I could barely see past the haze. It was like a surreal dream, a hideous nightmare. We took refuge in an open-pit air raid shelter. This was an extremely long and deep open tunnel in the ground where children and mothers with babies hid. The sides of the trench were covered with long grass and tall plants to help conceal us from the planes overhead.

I wished I were invisible as I crouched in the dirt. Just then, the firebombs began dropping from the sky like lethal rain with a deafening crashing sound that chilled my heart. I felt frozen and numb as I watched them fall like deadly stars wreaking havoc and devastation. I covered my mouth and nostrils with my hand so I wouldn't inhale the smoke. The heat was overwhelming.

My scalp was so itchy that I felt like it was burning. I was frightened when I saw white lice eggs in my jet black hair. I could see the other children crouching near me with thick scarves covering their mouths and their wide eyes glistening. They huddled together, trying not to cry. We were all terrified and weeping inwardly, but we wouldn't show our fear. It would cause distress to our mothers, who were standing near the front and forming a barrier, along with the man who was the head of the shelter. He was a stern, tall soldier wearing a green, moss-colored steel hat and bearing a rifle. Somehow it was comforting that he was there to protect us. We knew we were not alone.

I saw scurrying ants moving near me on the ground. They were even more helpless than we were. I wanted to protect the little ants, to save them, to be like the soldier who was watching over us. I realized then that everyone was protecting someone. There was always someone more helpless than us struggling to survive. This made me feel brave and old somehow.

There was smoke everywhere. I could hear the horrific crashing of the firebombs as they landed and I could see gigantic flames rising through the haze and debris flying through the air. Chaotic screams filled the air. I could barely see shadowy figures, like spirits, running and falling to the ground. Then it was still as their lives were extinguished. I held a scarf to my mouth and nose, trying not to inhale the toxic fumes. I knew their lives were passing with the vapors into the gray atmosphere beyond.

Suddenly the crashing stopped and all that was left was terrible silence punctuated by cries. Another air raid had passed. We lifted ourselves slowly from the dirt trench. Thick dust and smoke filled our lungs and eyes, choking and blinding us.

Numbly, through the haze, I surveyed the destruction. There was a sea of fire, rubble, and blood everywhere and hundreds of injured and lifeless bodies scattered like a mass grave. Nearby, people stood in a line, chattering senselessly, weeping quietly behind brave facades and passing along water buckets in systematic chains to extinguish the flames.

Japanese homes, traditionally constructed of wood and paper, ignited easily and burned like torches. A large piece of wood fell from the roof of a burning home, scattering sparks and red-hot embers before us. A frantic mother chased after her crying child, whose clothes were half torn and burnt. Attendants ran about madly, administering first aid. Ghostly women wearing air raid hoods were carrying stretchers and moving the blood-soaked wounded to first aid stations. Voices intermingled frantically, and the air was ringing with faceless cries of desperation and fear.

My mother grabbed my hand. I looked over her shoulder and saw a young, dead body lying on the ground soaked in a pool of dark blood. The boy's lifeless, glassy stare filled me with horror. It looked as though he had seen a ghost and died instantly of fright.

"Oka-chan, I'm scared," I cried. My entire body shook at the death and destruction around me, and I could barely see through the hot tears pouring from my eyes. I was completely exhausted. We hadn't slept or eaten for days.

"Mi-chan, *daijobu yo*, don't worry," she whispered comfortingly to me as we quickly left the area. Terrified, I buried my face in her shoulder, hiding from the horror that confronted me. I couldn't bear to see dead bodies strewn on the ground everywhere we looked—so much blood, limbs torn off, and faces disfigured. The sheer impact and scale of the destruction were staggering and horrific. So many innocent civilian lives had been extinguished instantly. What had they done to deserve this?

"Mi-chan, *isoide*, hurry, I need to see Hashimoto-san," she said. "I hope she is safe."

Quickly, we ran along partially destroyed city streets lined by stern soldiers, trying to maintain some semblance of order and authority. Some local people were compassionately tending to the wounded or helping others find their loved ones who had been lost in the chaos. I saw others searching through damaged homes with large sacks slung across their backs as they collected whatever they could salvage from the wreckage and ruins, even shards of pottery and the broken remains of other precious possessions. Others simply wandered, looking like lost souls, broken from the trauma and suffering.

Although it was quiet now, I sensed the imminent danger of being exposed and captured by the enemy. They could return again at any moment, without warning. This had happened so many times before when our false sense of security gave way as we were blindsided by another sudden attack. We could not afford to be complacent. I ran alongside my mother, driven by sheer determination despite my exhaustion and the fear that shook my very core.

"Do you need to rest, Mi-chan?" my mother turned to me with concern. She could sense my fatigue.

"Thank you, Oka-chan. I'm fine," I replied. "I hope your friend is safe."

"That's very thoughtful of you," my mother said kindly and smiled.

We continued along the winding streets until we emerged into a field with tall grass, bordered by houses in the distance. Somehow, we both sensed there was danger, and this was a very exposed area. There was nowhere to hide.

"You must be ready to run for cover at any moment, Mi-chan," my mother explained. "Stay close to me and don't let go of my hand."

"*Hai*, yes, Oka-chan," I nodded.

Suddenly, we heard the deafening sirens blaring again and then the thundering sound of a plane very close to us. We were caught in the middle of an air attack by a fierce B-29 plane, and we seemed to be at its epicenter, trapped in a field with no place to hide. Inside the menacing plane overhead, we knew there was one pilot and one gunner aiming at the people scattered below. The bullets were raining down in a deadly shower with tremendous noise.

"Now, quickly!" my mother shouted and squeezed my hand. "We need to find shelter." We were now in the middle of the grassy field, and I could barely see the houses in the distance. They were too far to reach in time, like a distant shore that seemed to be receding as we watched.

I ran as fast as my legs could carry me in sheer panic, knowing my life depended on it. I could feel my heart pounding within my chest—so hard I thought it would explode. Suddenly my mother tripped on a rock, fell hard on the ground, and lost my hand. I cried out to her, but the siren drowned out my frightened voice. I fell too, and my body hit the ground so hard I couldn't move from the shock for a moment. Yet I knew that my life might depend upon getting up again and escaping. I could feel the jagged rocks cutting my palms as I frantically pushed myself up from the ground. I couldn't see my mother anywhere. I stood entirely alone, shaking with terror. There was nowhere to hide. I felt like a rabbit in a field, pursued by hunters. I felt faint and the world seemed to spin around me. All I could see was the plane above and death everywhere around me. Darkness was descending upon me like mist. There was no escape.

"*Abu nai!* Danger! Get down!" I heard soldiers shouting. An old soldier tried to catch my leg to prevent me from standing. He threw himself in front of me to block me from the aerial attack. The roaring of the approaching bombers was deafening.

Ta-ta-ta-ta-ta! I heard the terrifying, staccato sound of gunfire so close to me that my ears were ringing from the noise. I felt ice cold, as though I were about to faint.

I suddenly felt an incredible weight as the soldier fell on me. The sheer force knocked me over, and I thought my body would shatter into a thousand pieces from the weight upon my small, frail frame. As I fell he crumpled to the ground beside me, completely lifeless. He had been shot and I could see bright blood oozing from where the bullet had fatally pierced his chest. I heard the thunderous plane right above me, signaling destruction. I opened my mouth to scream, but I couldn't make a sound. I was paralyzed with fear. Gunshots reverberated around me and people scattered, screamed, and fell to the ground. The noise was absolutely deafening. I held my hands to my ears and knelt beside the still soldier, pretending to myself that I was hiding safely in an air raid shelter beside my mother, rather than out in the open alone. I thought of the ants. I would protect them too. My heart was palpitating so quickly that I felt like it was going to burst and I was about to die. After several tense minutes, I sensed that the danger was over. The plane had passed over us and disappeared.

The cloud of smoke and dust obscured my vision. I blinked and my heart leaped as suddenly I saw my mother running frantically toward me, tears streaming down her face and sheer panic in her dark eyes. She flung her arms around me desperately and held me so tightly I thought she would never let me go.

"Mi-chan, I'm so sorry I lost your hand." My mother was sobbing. "The plane was shooting at us and I couldn't find you. You were saved by that old soldier. He shielded you from the gunfire with his body."

My mother bowed so low toward the soldier's body that her head was touching the dirt, to show him the greatest respect and honor, and she said a silent prayer. I followed her example and bowed so low that my forehead was covered in dirt.

She hugged me again and said, "He saved your life, Mi-chan. What a brave man. I am so grateful." We both sat on the ground beside the man's limp, lifeless body. His eyes were closed in his thin, worn face, and he wore the soldier's familiar dark green uniform, now stained with blood.

"He had goodness and purity in his soul," she said. "His life ended just as a flower gets cut. His noble sacrifice has ensured the safety of your life. His soul is now traveling to the Pure Land, where he will have eternal life."

People arrived with a stretcher then and took him away. I realized that I could never thank him for saving my life. I was crying so hard my body was shaking. He didn't even know my name, and I would never know his. For the first time, I felt the war had changed the course of my life. My mother and I sat for long time in silence, staring at the spot where he had fallen. I had never personally experienced death before. Now life and death existed side by side. Death had touched me with its icy hand, but I had been spared.

I was still terrified to move. The planes might attack again. Somehow I couldn't bring myself to leave that hallowed spot where the soldier had died, knowing I would never find it again or be able to mark the significance of that place in my life. A single bullet extinguished a brave man's life in front of me after his spontaneous act of kindness. I had received the ultimate gift of generosity and love. I sobbed in anguish and gratitude for his noble sacrifice.

"I will never forget this," I cried. "Thank you, thank you, thank you! I promise I will repay your gift someday."

The rain started to fall. My mother said this meant his soul would have a safe journey to heaven. We bowed low again in silence. Suddenly, the blaring siren cried out, warning us that another attack was on the horizon.

"We must go, Mi-chan," my mother said gently, but there was a sense of urgency in her voice. "It isn't safe to remain here."

I held her hand and we ran as fast as we could. I felt like we were flying across that nightmarish landscape. We needed to find her friend so we ran past the dead bodies, the wall of flames, and the mothers who had lost loved ones, consumed by grief. I couldn't see the sun. It was as though it had deserted us and left us in this gray, smoky wasteland of burnt corpses. Even the grass looked gray. I kept thinking that it ought to have been me, that I should be the one lying dead on a stretcher.

Suddenly I woke up. My face was covered in tears and I was shaking uncontrollably. My teeth were chattering like old times during the war.

"Oka-chan," I cried, "the soldier is gone! I didn't get to thank him."

"You are safe now, Mi-chan," my mother said softly, comforting me in my confusion. "We are at Hanaokayama. The war is over."

My shallow, frantic breathing slowed as the realization dawned up me. "Really? We're safe?"

"Yes," my mother reassured me. "We're very safe, Mi-chan. We must pray for the soldier's soul and never forget that he gave you the most precious and extraordinary gift. He gave his own life to save yours."

"How can I thank him?" I asked, distraught. "He is gone forever."

"You must always show *kansha* and he will know that you appreciate his sacrifice. He was a true samurai warrior who fell in battle like a cherry blossom and gave his life to save a stranger without hesitation. I am eternally grateful he saved you. He knew that your life was a treasure."

"He was so brave," I sobbed. "He didn't even know me, but he saved me."

"Mi-chan, you must live every day fully and be fearless and strong for him," she replied. "He gave you the gift of life and love. Your gift to him is your strength and courage. He knew your life was worth saving."

She hugged me and I knew she was right. I could be courageous like him, and I would always appreciate his sacrifice. In that moment, I promised never to waste my life. It was a precious gift he died to save. I had vowed to him that I would repay his kindness someday, and I would never forget that promise.

Every time I see a cherry blossom falling, I think of his fearlessness and glory in choosing death to save my life. Our destinies are forever inextricably linked. Whenever I face adversity, I tell myself to stand up and live the life he gave me. I owe it to him and to my mother.

Life is fleeting like *sakura*, the cherry blossom,
so live wisely and courageously.

CHAPTER 3

TAKARA / TREASURE

I was still trembling when I opened my eyes. The warm sun penetrated through the translucent white shoji doors, casting a protective band of light around me. I suddenly realized where I was. It was remarkable to think that the brave soldier's kindness of spirit had helped transport me to this safe and splendid world.

As I touched the floor, I felt the woven tatami mat beneath me. This uniquely Japanese invention is made of layers of tightly woven rice straw made up of intricate strands. These mats formed the backdrop of our lives.

My mother taught me that more than 10,000 years ago, an ancient god created Japan, sending us a brother god and sister goddess. These two created the islands of Japan and became the source of the nation's spirit. This was Shinto, meaning "the way of the gods." These beings imbued everything natural—both living and inanimate things—with kami, special spirits that flowed through and connected all things. I was amazed that everything I saw with my eyes had a unique spirit. As I felt the tatami mat beneath me, I thought that even this had a spirit, since it was made of rice straw, and rice grew with the divine help of Amaterasu, the ancient sun goddess believed to be an ancestor of the Imperial family.

I looked at our simple room and sighed with relief. At last I found myself in a place where I felt that no destructive power could ever reach us. I could hear the birds chirping and the mystical chanting of monks in the distance. The combination of sounds was soothing to my mind and body. The wind carried this rare music aloft, causing gentle movement in the flowers, leafy trees, and shrubberies. All of nature was in harmony in this moment. We were enveloped by this melody that seemed to wrap around us like a silk ribbon and bind us together.

"*Ohayo gozaimasu*, good morning," my mother said, gently sliding open the shoji door. It was reassuring to hear her clear voice echo in this room like the ringing of a bell. She always had a soft but commanding voice and an air of effortless grace.

"How is my *takara*, my treasure?" she asked with a smile. "Did you sleep well after your nightmare?"

"Yes, Oka-chan, much better." I replied. "It's so quiet here. I can hear the sparrows singing. I'd like to fly above the mountain like they do. They must see everything."

"Later we can go for a walk," my mother said. "When you walk on Hanaokayama, you will feel like you are flying. You can see so much below. Why don't you wash your face? Then we can have breakfast."

When I returned to the house, I saw small dishes on the veranda.

My mother handed me an *oshibori*, a small warm towel, so I could clean my hands before we ate.

"Thank you, Oka-chan," I said. "What pretty dishes!"

"Aren't they wonderful?" she said, smiling. "The priest said we could use them. We are so fortunate."

We had a small portion of root vegetables, which looked so dainty on the plates. It was as though the plate were framing the food, like art. After I finished eating, I sat outside with my mother.

"Mi-chan, today we are going to the *ohaka*," she said as she gently brushed my hair. The ohaka is a grave in an ancient Buddhist temple in Kumamoto where my ancestors' ashes lay protected under a large stone. My father's family had been living in Kumamoto for generations. They were descendants of samurai warriors.

"We must visit your father and thank him for finding such a tranquil place to stay," she told me. "He would be so happy to see you safe, smiling, and strong. You have always been our *takara*, our treasure. You are filled with the gifts and talents of your ancestors. There is no one else in the world like you. Remember—you have a special destiny to fulfill."

This gave me pause. "What *is* my destiny, Oka-chan?" I asked her.

"That is for you to discover, Mi-chan," she replied. "I am sure you will have many adventures in the future. This is only the beginning of an exciting journey for you."

"It does seem like something magical has brought us here," I agreed, looked around me. "I wish father could see this place. I'm sure he would like it."

"You are a very thoughtful girl, Mi-chan," my mother said approvingly. "Why don't you gather some wildflowers to bring him? You could take some of the spirit of the mountain to him."

I remembered how my mother used to buy flowers and special incense to take to the ohaka. I knew that things had changed after the war, but I thought that delicate blossoms from this mountain would be worthy of decorating my father's grave.

"I'd love to do that," I agreed. "Then every day when he admires the flowers, he will share our view." I couldn't wait to show him how unique this place was.

"Remember," my mother warned, "you can pick wildflowers so long as you plan to use them respectfully. There is no higher purpose than to beautify the house of your ancestors and show *kansha* for your father's memory."

"Thank you, Oka-chan," I replied.

I ran to greet my tree friends, and my feet pressed lightly into the buoyant grass. I could feel the breeze in my hair, and I twirled around joyously. I stopped and bowed deeply to the trees.

"I am going to the *ohaka* today," I told them proudly.

Leaves fluttered their reply on the breeze.

I returned to where my mother sat and told her I was going near the well to gather some flowers. She nodded and smiled.

"Be careful on the steps, Mi-chan!" she called after me.

"*Hai*, yes," I called back. "I'll be careful!"

I wandered down to the well, where an abundance of verdant plants and wildflowers created a fragrant palette of cream and pink blossoms, swirling among a nest of lush dark green. I closed my eyes and inhaled the pure fragrance. It transported me to the immaculate gardens of my home before the war. My mother told me we had indoor servants and outdoor servants. My brother, who was ten years older, remembered the lavish parties our parents hosted and hearing my mother's voice floating through the corridors when she sang. In the years after the war, I heard many nostalgic stories about our old home, and it became an almost mythical place to me—like a palace in a fairytale. I wish I could remember it.

"*Ohayo gozaimasu!*" I greeted the flowers and plants respectfully, bowing as I remembered my mother's words. "I would like you to help me honor my ancestors and decorate our ohaka. I want to share this magical mountain with them and show them that I am safe here with you now that the war is over."

I wanted the flowers to know how special this grave was. "You have to climb many steep steps to reach the main gravestone," I explained. "The stone has our family name. The *ohaka* has a tree of its own, too, standing very tall and touching the sky. There is green moss on the ground, and nearby there are small, delicate wildflowers. I call them 'Momo-chan' since they are pink! I want to take some of you back to the *ohaka* to show my ancestors what a magnificent, peaceful place we are living in now."

I heard the subtle sound of rustling among the flowers. I took this as a sign of their approval, and gently plucked enough flowers to create two small bouquets.

"I shall take you to represent Hanaokayama to my ohaka," I respectfully told the blooms in my hands. "*Domo arigato gozaimasu.* Thank you very much."

I bowed low for a long time in gratitude, remembering that we are all connected and that all things in nature have a spirit. I felt that the flowers and plants understood my kansha. They knew they would honor my ancestors.

As I carefully held the bouquets, a dainty white butterfly fluttered past. Its translucent wings were like the petals of the cherry blossoms, and it flitted gracefully past me before disappearing into the glowing sky. I knew it was a sign. My mother taught me the butterfly represents the spirit of our ancestors.

"Oka-chan!" I almost tripped in my excitement as I ran to show my mother the bouquets. "I saw a white butterfly after I gathered them. I know it's a sign!"

"These are the most wonderful arrangements I have ever seen," my mother replied. "I think you are right, Mi-chan. Our ancestors *must* be pleased."

She smiled gently, "*Sa-a, ikimasho*, come, let's go."

I felt so proud. My mother said I had made *wonderful* bouquets. The flowers that I chose from the mountain had earned our ancestors' approval.

As my mother and I walked together down the hill, I was amazed to find that the road before us was as white as snow—carpeted in fresh flowers. The cherry blossoms were blooming gloriously, and their pristine petals fluttered down from the sky like snowflakes. I opened my arms wide to feel each silken petal and appreciate its ephemeral beauty as each one pirouetted down to the earth. I couldn't help dancing.

"Oka-chan, how beautiful!" I exclaimed. "They are dancing with me."

I never dreamt I would know this kind of beauty after the war. Each petal seemed to have its own spirit, and every one was falling from the sky just to dance with me.

My mother hugged me. "Each day is a new gift for you," she said. "Enjoy these moments, Mi-chan. They are gifts to be treasured."

The mountain seemed alive. Bursts of petals rained from the sky, creating intricate patterns on the grass like fine embroidery on a kimono. The mountain was changing into her finest garments for spring, like a bride.

"Mi-chan, *hanami*," she said, speaking the word with intention. "Have I told you about how the tradition of flower viewing began?" she asked.

"No," I said, shaking my head. I looked around, "But I could see why everyone would want to look at them."

"They are so stunning, but they bloom for such a short time," she explained. "The blossoms fade so quickly that, a long time ago, the Imperial Court was inspired to start the tradition of viewing the cherry blossoms. Under the sakura trees, they all had a lavish lunch, drank sake, and danced. It was a celebration of the fleeting beauty of these blossoms, which became an annual tradition. Both rich and poor would unite in their appreciation of the cherry blossoms. We are all part of nature, and like the blossoms we, too, have limited time here on earth."

"Did you have a celebration here?" I asked.

"Your father always held a large gathering in our gardens for the people from his company and their families," she replied. "It was a wonderful occasion, which everyone looked forward to each year. They would admire the blossoms, and we would serve them delicacies on our finest china and lacquerware." She looked thoughtful and distant. I could almost see these times of luxury and civility reflected in her dark eyes, lost to her now.

"I wish I could have seen them," I said softly. I looked at her again, wanting to catch a glimpse of that past I would never know.

"Mi-chan," she smiled. "Be grateful that you can see them now. Flowers teach us so much about life and appreciation. We used to sing a special song when we admired the falling sakura blossoms. Can you guess what it was?"

"Sakura!" I cried. It was my mother's favorite song.

As we walked and absorbed the beauty around us, I noticed that the cherry trees, lining the road from the top of the mountain all the way down to the bottom, looked like soldiers saluting the emperor.

I held my mother's hand, and she sang to me as we strolled. Her tinkling voice captivated even the flower petals, which seemed to stop to admire the song about their beauty. I joined in the singing, too. As we walked slowly down the hill, I felt as though I had been transformed into a sakura blossom myself, gently descending from the sky and floating along the breeze like the notes of our song. The blossoms like falling snow were a reminder of the old soldier's gift of courage and how his valiant act had saved my life.

I looked up at the dancing blossoms, in awe of that perfect and ephemeral moment before they fell to the ground forever. I danced with them in appreciation of their eternal beauty, grace, and the strength of their spirit that would never fade.

We arrived at the temple where my ancestors' ashes were interred in our family grave. It was surrounded by ancient pine trees and gardens that were so still they seemed deserted. The temple had been spared from the devastation of the air raids and remained unchanged. This place held such a profound sense of permanence that it made me forget this was the same city I saw ravaged by war, and which haunted my dreams.

I went to the well and pumped water into a bucket. Carefully carrying the bucket of water we would use to wash the grave, I climbed up the steps leading to the gray stone marker bearing our family's name. Reverentially, I arranged the bouquets of wildflowers. My mother lit the incense we had brought from the temple on the flower mountain. The moment I smelled its sweet fragrance, I was transported to the top of the mountain, which flashed vividly in my mind. I felt our ancestors were with us as my mother performed purification rituals to honor the deceased.

I knelt again before the worn stone marker with my mother, thanking my father and our ancestors for our life and the house on the mountain. I told them that I had brought the flowers so I could share the enchanted mountain's beauty with them. As I expressed my gratitude, I felt a sense of warmth, and a gentle wind made the plants and flowers sway. I sensed that they appreciated being in such a glorious place, paying respect to my ancestors. I promised them that I would come back often to visit.

The temple priest was a tall and stern-looking man. He greeted us and recited Buddhist sutras as he sounded the *mokugyo*, a round wooden fish that he hit with a mallet, at the altar. The instrument made a clear, haunting, hollow sound as he struck the wood repeatedly with the mallet, keeping time with his rhythmic chanting. We felt honored to hear such a profound prayer for our venerable ancestors. The deep sound of the mokugyo resonated in our hearts and helped us focus on this solemn act of remembrance. I felt the spirits of our ancestors were surrounding us closely as we prayed.

As we prepared to depart after the ceremony was complete, I looked back wistfully at my flower friends and the solid gray stone. I knew they would be happy there. I said goodbye to my father and my ancestors and bowed very low. I remembered my mother's words that I was her takara, filled with my ancestors' gifts and talents. I silently thanked them for these gifts, and I promised that I would honor their memory by being strong and dutiful.

As we walked back along the road, my mother explained we needed to go past the train station in the town for our food rations. My heart sank when I remembered the deafening sirens, air raids, and leaping flames.

As we walked through the town, I thought about the momentous day I went to our local shrine with my mother to hear the emperor give a speech over the radio, surrendering to the Allied forces. We were kneeling on the ground with our heads bowed so low they nearly touched the dirt. The Japanese remained loyal to the emperor even in this humbling moment of defeat.

The soldiers in uniform around us shouted a resounding refrain, both euphoric and tragic: "*Banzai, banzai, banzai!*"

The word was invented about a hundred years before, during the Meiji period when Japan opened its ports to the world, rapidly modernizing and defeating both China and Russia. "Banzai" means "1,000 years." It came to be used when good fortune occurs, such as at weddings or sporting events. On the day the emperor surrendered, it was bittersweet. Foreigners had defeated the Japanese, but our people's pride could not be diminished.

After the war came the American occupation, during which American personnel supervised government officials and dictated every aspect of life in Japan. The government issued each family a license to obtain what little food was available. We were so hungry and dirty. They sprayed DDT on our heads to kill the lice in our hair. The toxic chemicals made my nostrils burn. I remember cringing, hoping the lice wouldn't move down my head and that I wouldn't inhale the fumes. I heard a popping sound like a gun going off as I was sprayed with the white chemical powder. I couldn't see until someone gave me a tissue to wipe the stinging powder off my face. No matter how much I wiped my face and neck, the horrible odor permeated every pore.

It was strange to reflect back on these events now, as I passed familiar scenes and saw American soldiers at their posts. As we reached the train station, I saw a long line of Japanese soldiers wearing white robes like ghosts. Some were on crutches and some only had one arm or one leg. Numbly, I stared around me at the food line as we joined it. One by one, the people were served a small ration by the government agents. They took their parcel, bowed, and left obediently.

An extremely thin young woman with long black hair and fearful, dark eyes stood behind us, holding a crying baby in her arms. Her eyes looked so large in her gaunt, pale face. There was a haunting look that spoke of deep suffering and irreparable loss. She tried to comfort her baby, but the little one wouldn't stop wailing.

Eventually it was our turn to receive our food.

"Please go in front of us, poor baby," my mother told the young woman with a gentle smile. "She is your *takara*. Please let her have food so she can grow strong."

The mother thanked us tearfully many times and bowed very low in respect to my mother. "Thank you so much." Her voice trembled and broke. "She weeps for her father."

My mother's eyes glistened with tears, and she gently touched the woman's hand.

An aid worker comforted the woman and said, "Sit here, I will find something for your baby."

When it was our turn, we were handed a burlap sack with our allocation of food. My mother accepted it, thanked the agent, and bowed politely. As we carried our precious rations from the American food service home, I was comforted by the thought that we would have a warm dinner. I peeked into the sack and saw the familiar sight of sweet potatoes with their reddish brown skin. I sighed. I missed rice so much. I don't remember when we last had it. I often secretly thought of having bowls of fresh, steaming hot rice. Rice was such a staple of the Japanese diet. We hadn't realized what a luxury it was until the war came and it became a scarce commodity.

As we walked, I noticed my mother looked very tired. Her bun had come loose and her gold glasses slipped down her nose as she walked. She was still smiling, but I noticed that her eyes looked weary.

"Oka-chan, the sweet potatoes look delicious. Isn't it nice that we can have some hot food?" I asked. "I saved some onions from before. We can have those, too."

"We are very lucky to have food, Mi-chan," she added. "The sweet potatoes are full of vitamins and will help you grow strong."

We walked along the road and saw some familiar faces from the city. They brightened in recognition as they saw us, too. They were all trying to rebuild their homes piece by piece. Our old neighbors were putting up worn cloth to divide the rooms where shoji screens had once stood. Everybody was helping each other and speaking cheer-fully. I felt so proud to be part of such a community of kind people with such a sense of determination. They could see a brighter future, even when it was hardest to see. They believed they could rebuild our country again. I thought of the resilient strands of the tatami and the rice straw bending in the wind. Their spirits could not be broken, not even by war and deep loss.

There was a woman handing out small pieces of cooked sweet pota-toes to help feed her hungry neighbors. The sweet smell wafted in the air and made my stomach rumble. Now I was grateful for the sweet potatoes in our little burlap sack. She offered some to my mother.

"Thank you so much," my mother said and bowed low with respect. "We appreciate your kindness, but we have just received our parcel of food."

As we continued down the main road, an elderly woman took a towel and put it on my neck. "Please keep this, dear Mi-chan," she said. "I just washed it. Please help your mother. She looks tired." I bowed in gratitude, and my mother smiled.

Another lady handed me some flatbread. It was warm in my hands and the delicious aroma filled my nostrils. She smiled and said, "Be a good girl and take care of your mother. When I see you again, I might give you cookies or candy." I bowed again, with tears in my eyes. Her gen-erosity was astonishing. She was willing to give us what little food she had.

We passed the townspeople and proceeded toward the incline of the mountain. My mother was walking very slowly. She seemed unsteady on her feet, as though it were a struggle to walk.

"Would you like to rest for a while?" I asked her. "It's been a long walk. I'm feeling tired, too."

"Thank you, Mi-chan," my mother replied. "Why don't we go the other way to return home? The stairs will be easier to climb and we can rest along the way."

I could see my mother making a concerted effort to keep pace with me as we walked, even though I had slowed down considerably.

"Great!" I replied. "We will have a different view from the steps. I'd love to see the ancient stone staircase."

All the stones that formed the stairway leading to Hanaokayama were chiseled by hand. It was a marvel of human construction that enabled travelers to climb to the top of the mountain. The sides of the venerable stones were covered with thick green moss. It looked so alive with its vivid color and intricate pattern. Our path was flanked by lush, tall trees, which made the road quite dark even in the daytime. It was so still. The cool breeze passed us and we felt like we were in the middle of a forest. We took each step carefully, one by one. I looked back anxiously at my mother to ensure she wasn't getting too tired to climb the steps.

"I wonder how they built these steps originally," I said. "Imagine how much time it must have taken."

My mother walked alongside me slowly. She replied, "They must have been very patient. They knew what they were building would last for a very long time and would help many weary travelers reach the top of the mountain."

"Are you all right, Oka-chan?" I asked her. "You must be so hungry. I will make you a lovely lunch. We will have this warm bread and fresh potatoes."

"You are such a kind girl, Mi-chan," my mother replied. "You are always thinking of others. I am so proud of you. I think we can save our food for dinner. We must be careful not to eat it too quickly. It will need to last for several days."

I nodded. She was always very sensible.

"Mi-chan, I spoke to your headmistress," my mother said. "She will be providing some books for you to read, so you won't fall behind in your studies. She is worried about your health and agrees you should gain your strength here before coming back to school."

I knew I would rather be here than at school for lessons. It was so much more exciting to be learning under the sky with the soaring birds and dancing cherry blossoms. Even now, I felt as though we were in a fairytale, ascending into a mystical land in the sky. The ancient trees were like giants around us, and this stone path might lead to the stars.

The sunlight hit our feet as we reached the clearing at the top of the steps. We had emerged from the dark forest into glorious sunshine. This was the top of the mountain. We had returned home safely. Glowing light reflected off the roof of our little house, which appeared illuminated in its protective circle of tall trees. When I saw it my heart leaped. I knew this was our home.

The view of the lilac and green valley below us was dotted with white blossoms. The mountain was picturesque in the soft haze of the afternoon.

"Do you hear how the birds are singing more loudly than before?" my mother asked me as we took in the stunning view. "That means spring is here. They know the blossoms have arrived and that the mountains and fields are being transformed. They are calling to each other."

"They know the season is changing," I said. "They're so clever!"

"Yes," my mother agreed. "The birds have already built their nests and laid their eggs. Soon we will see little chicks hatching and hear their new songs. Treasure all of this, Mi-chan, every view, every blossom, every birdsong. We are so fortunate to be surrounded by nature's beauty everywhere. We must always see and appreciate it. Every day should be a celebration of life."

We sang joyfully as we walked up to the house, expressing the exhilaration we felt at the arrival of spring and the sense of jubilation that seemed to resonate on this mountain, in the sky above, and all around us.

You are a unique *takara*, treasure, and there
is no one like you in the world.

四

CHAPTER 4

UMI / SEA

The morning was quiet and the sunlight glowed on the mountain and the tall, swaying trees. My mother and brother had gone to the countryside a few days before to exchange her fine silk kimono for some more food and supplies for us. It had been a wedding gift from her father, a wealthy merchant in Nagasaki. Ever since the war, my mother had been selling her kimonos to help us survive. These were the only reminders of our former luxury and of her late parents. They were the only valuable items we had left, since everything else had been destroyed during the war. She looked wistful as I watched her fold up the intricately embroidered silk so gently, as though she were parting with the treasured memories of her youth.

My mother and I walked to the highest point of the mountain where we could see the city. This was our favorite place to walk. It had the best view of the valley and the hills. As the priest had advised, we embraced this form of walking meditation, and it helped us to clear our minds and become one with the nature surrounding us. We immersed ourselves fully in this extraordinary landscape. Everything looked small and faded from our vantage point on Hanaokayama, and I saw a new view of the world. It was exhilarating to float above the city like a soaring hawk. I felt I could touch the endless sapphire sky and the sweeping clouds that looked like cotton. My mother was right. It *was* like flying, and I felt completely free.

"Mi-chan, this is an incredible view. It's very different from the one I had from my home in Nagasaki," my mother said as she surveyed the scene. "Imagine if all these hills below us were transformed into deep blue waves and the trees into mighty wooden ships with billowing white sails like these clouds above. I remember the thrill of seeing the tall ships in the harbor. There was such a sense of adventure and endless possibilities."

"It must have been so exciting," I said. I closed my eyes and imagined the busy harbor and sailors rushing about.

"It was, Mi-chan," she agreed. "It was a perfect place to grow up. I dreamed of sailing to see the world. I would often walk past the harbor to school and wonder where the ships would be sailing next. The view was always changing and the harbor reflected the vibrant colors of the city. In the morning, the rising golden sun reflected off of the water, and in the evening the harbor glowed with the flickering lights."

"Where did the ships travel?" I asked.

"All over the world," she replied. "Nagasaki is an international city. For more than 200 years, it was the only port in Japan that was open to foreign trade. Dutch and Portuguese merchants and sailors came to trade beautiful and exotic things from around the world. The ships still transport goods throughout the world—everything from silk to tobacco to *castella*, my favorite cake and one of Nagasaki's delicacies. *Bunmeido castella* is very famous. It's the finest castella in the world, so delicate, light, and golden. Portuguese merchants originally brought castella to Nagasaki and taught the Japanese how to make it."

It was difficult to imagine my mother being small like me and going to school every day, skipping along and daydreaming about adventures and eating castella.

"What was your school like, Oka-chan?" I asked.

"I went to Kwassui Women's College. I was very happy there," she explained. "I studied literature, music, and history. I had very kind friends. My parents encouraged me to sing and read Japanese books and Western books, too. I learned about all the famous composers. Puccini was my favorite. I always wrote and painted with a brush and ink."

I admired how gracefully my mother painted, as though the brush were an extension of her hand. The precision of each brushstroke was astonishing. This was the result of years of practice and discipline writing calligraphy and painting with watercolors. In the tradition of Japanese calligraphy and painting, you cannot disguise mistakes by painting over them. Each line or wash of color must be laid down perfectly the first time, or else the scroll is ruined.

"That's how you learned to paint such incredible pictures," I said.

"Yes," she replied. "I loved art and music. My teachers inspired me so much. I wanted to practice every day so I would constantly improve and become like the great masters I admired. I wanted to be able to capture the essence of the city I loved with a brush."

"You seemed so happy in Nagasaki," I said. "You didn't want to stay there?"

"As I looked out at the harbor, my mind was completely free," she told me. "I would dream of exploring the world. But I knew my parents would make plans for me. I was the youngest of four daughters, and my parents wanted to ensure I had a comfortable future. I came here with my nursemaid after my father arranged my marriage to your father."

I thought about what it must have been like for my mother to be told whom she was to marry.

"Your father had been married before but his wife passed away," she continued. "He was nearly seventeen years older than me. I remember how proud my mother was that he was descended from samurai warriors in Kumamoto. Your father's family has lived here for generations and is very distinguished. Your grandfather was loyal to the Tokugawa shogunate, which ended in 1867 when Emperor Meiji resumed Imperial rule of Japan. The samurai lost much of their power under Imperial rule."

"Was it difficult for my father and his family after the shogun was defeated?" I asked.

"Fortunately for your father, your grandmother was a very strong-willed and independent lady," my mother said. "Unlike your grandfather, her family had sided with the Imperial powers, not with the shogun. She lived on a local lord's large private estate, which was destroyed by the shogun's supporters. She fled to Kumamoto with her nursemaid when she was young. The whole country was very unstable, and her family suffered for supporting the emperor instead of the traditional feudal lords. There was a short period of civil war until the emperor was restored to power in 1868. Then your father and his mother were held in favor for their support of the new emperor."

"What was it like moving to Kumamoto?" I asked my mother.

"It was so different from Nagasaki," my mother said. "I missed my old life and the bay very much, but your father had a grand house with exquisite gardens and loyal servants. His mother—your grandmother— was a very elegant woman, like the refined ladies in traditional court paintings. Her skin was fair and flawless like porcelain. Her movements were so graceful and controlled, cultivated and refined."

I thought of the traditional court paintings my mother referred to. I had seen them in books before the war. I loved the illustrations in my book about the tragic fairytale of *Kaguya-hime*, Princess Kaguya, the moon princess who was found by a farmer in the stalk of a bamboo plant. After being raised by the farmer and his wife, she was forced to return home to her family on the moon. The book had colorful, stylized paintings from the seventeenth century. The ladies were the embodiment of refinement with their pale skin, long, black hair and fine silk kimonos that seemed to flow behind them like ethereal waterfalls of cascading silk. In other books I read, traditional noblewomen always had artistic and musical accomplishments. They would kneel and play the *koto*, the Japanese harp with thirteen strings. It had a haunting, otherworldly sound. I admired the women who could play it so flawlessly, as though their hands were floating over the strings to create shimmering notes.

"What was my grandmother like?" I asked. "Was she kind?"

"She was very gracious," my mother replied. "However, I think she wished I had not been a merchant's daughter. She never said it, since she was a lady, but I could sense it from the way she spoke of my father's trade. She was very proud of their family's heritage, and she was fond of his first wife. We had a lovely wedding in Nagasaki, though, and both of our families were there."

"What is a traditional wedding like, Oka-chan?" I asked with curiosity. I had never been to a Shinto wedding, but I had heard so much about the ceremony.

"I will try to describe it simply to you from what I remember. The bride wears an *uchikake*, a beautifully embroidered white and gold wedding kimono that symbolizes the sun's rays, two layers of robes underneath, and a *tsunokakushi*, a white silk headdress," my mother explained. "At the shrine, the priest performs a purification ritual by waving a *harai-gushi*, a ceremonial wand. He announces the marriage and asks the *kami* to bless it. There are three beautiful lacquerware sake cups of different sizes. The bride and groom drink three sips of sake from each cup. This tradition is called *san-san-kudo*. The groom reads his marriage vows. He and his bride make offerings of *tamagushi*, the branch of a sacred tree."

"It sounds very serious," I said.

"It is," she replied. "It's a very solemn and beautiful ceremony. I was very happy when I married your father, but it was difficult to say good-bye to my life and home in Nagasaki. I knew that this was the end of my old life and the beginning of a new life."

"It must have been such a change coming here," I said. Even with this magnificent view, I sensed it must be a contrast to the harbor with grand ships, sailors, and twinkling lights on the water.

"It was, but then we had such joyous news. Your father was so delighted when you were born. He said you had the samurai spirit of your ancestors, and he chose your name." She smiled and looked thoughtful. "Your name means 'fulfillment.' Your naming ceremony took seven days."

I knew what happened next. I had heard the story many times, and I often thought about how so much had changed for my mother and I, and how swiftly. A month later, I was taken to the Shinto shrine and blessed by a priest, a rite of passage known as *Omiyamairi*. My father died suddenly that same afternoon from a brain hemorrhage at the age of fifty-five. In quick succession, my mother's parents passed away as well, leaving her even more grief-stricken.

In need of help, my mother entrusted my father's friend and colleague with the management of his considerable estate. But my father's old friend turned out to be a duplicitous man who sold my father's estate and absconded to Manchuria with our family's fortune, never to be seen again. We were left virtually penniless, and we couldn't afford to pay the workers on the estate. Without wages they were unable to support their families and had to leave. Then of course the war came and tore our lives in Kumamoto apart. My mother's beloved Nagasaki was devastated by an atomic bomb that killed thousands of people instantly and left thousands more terminally ill from the radiation. After such a promising beginning and a safe and sheltered upbringing, so much unexpected tragedy had befallen my mother.

"I am so sorry for how you have suffered since then, Mi-chan," my mother told me softly, tears in her eyes as though she could read my thoughts. "I wish you could have known your father. I know he is proud of you. I'm so grateful that we have a safe home now, and that you can grow strong again."

"Oka-chan, please don't cry," I said as I hugged my mother tightly. "I am happy now."

I wished I could remember my father and recall his face. I had heard so many stories about him, but whenever I thought of him, there was a void. He was a missing memory. There was simply darkness, and when I dreamed of him, his face was blurred and anonymous.

"You must remember that you are our *takara*, our treasure. Then you can always be strong, even if you are alone. You made your father and I so happy when you were born," she said and hugged me again. "I am so thankful that you are my daughter."

"I will, Oka-chan," I promised. "Thank you for taking care of me. I'd like to learn more about Nagasaki. And I promise to have a traditional Shinto wedding when I am married someday."

"You will look beautiful, Mi-chan," my mother said. "I will be so proud to see you at your wedding." Though her words were happy, my mother looked sad and thoughtful. I wondered why, but I did not dare ask.

"Nagasaki sounds like a very special place," I said instead.

"It is," she agreed, her voice lifting. "It's such a unique city. I must take you to see it, Mi-chan. I want to show you the place where I spent my happiest times as a child. I treasure all of my memories from my youth in the city. It is a place which still remains in my heart."

"Are we going to Nagasaki?" my eyes widened in disbelief as I remembered the tales of destruction caused by the bomb and the thousands of people who had died. I had never seen it before, although I had heard my mother speak about the city often.

"Yes," my mother confirmed with a radiant smile. "I wanted to tell you, but it was a surprise. I have arranged train tickets for us, and our family will be waiting to see you." I could tell she was eager to share the news.

"I can't believe we're going to Nagasaki!" I cried. "That's amazing! I want to see the harbor and the ships."

"So you shall, Mi-chan," she said. "I will show you all my favorite places where I walked as a girl."

A few days later, we went to the train station early in the morning. I didn't see any soldiers there, though people were everywhere, busily rushing around the station. I held onto my ticket tightly, feeling that I was about to discover a special secret. In my other hand, I held a bouquet of wildflowers that I had picked for my cousin. Soon we boarded the train for Nagasaki, and the city of Kumamoto swept past the train windows until it became as blurry as a watercolor painting—blotches of green, gray, and blue in the morning mist.

I was so excited to see where my mother was born. I knew that the war had destroyed her family's sprawling home near the harbor with its view of the tall ships, but I had heard her describe the place so often that I felt like I knew it.

My uncle met us at the station. He was a tall, distinguished-looking man, but he didn't resemble my mother. He was cold and more reserved. Although he smiled kindly at me, his eyes held a deep sadness. He helped us into the car before driving us to his home just outside the city.

We found ourselves in a large, warm room with a fine tatami mat and the welcoming scent of food. We were greeted by my aunt's kind face. She was young but seemed careworn and anxious, with deep lines and shadows framing her dark eyes. She brought us warm bowls of soup made from fish stock and seaweed. The fresh scent reminded us that we were in a city by the harbor.

My mother looked very relaxed and happy. It was so reassuring to see her smiling again.

My aunt explained that their daughter, my cousin Teruko, was very weak and resting in bed. By the sorrowful look in her eyes as she spoke of her, I could tell that she was ill and not long for this world. My mother had told me that she, like thousands of others, suffered from radiation caused by the atomic bomb. She had leukemia, and there was nothing the doctors could do to save her.

I wanted to lift the sorrowful mood, so I spoke to my aunt about our little flower mountain and the cherry blossoms and magnificent trees. This made her smile and she listened to my tales with great interest.

"The mountain seems to change color every day," I explained. "Like she is wearing a different outfit or has a different mood. Today she was silvery and covered in mist when we were leaving to catch our train. Tomorrow she will be wearing white blossoms like the May queen."

"I'm so happy for you, Mi-chan," my aunt said. "You sound like you have a very comfortable home on Hanaokayama."

"It is the most wonderful place I've ever seen," I said. "You can see the whole city from the mountain, and I feel like I'm soaring with the birds among the clouds!"

As my aunt and I spoke about Kumamoto, my mother and uncle seemed to be having a quiet, intense conversation in the corner of the room. As I watched, suddenly my mother knelt and bowed very formally to him. My uncle bowed in return. They looked very serious. I wondered what they could be discussing. They spoke in such hushed tones that I couldn't hear them at all.

When we brought the visit to an end so my mother and I could catch the return train home, it seemed that the hours had passed so quickly. It was time to say goodbye.

"Please excuse us, we must return home today," my mother said as she bowed low to them. "It was so lovely to see you both. Thank you so much for your hospitality and kindness."

"Thank you, Masuko-san," my aunt replied. "We are so happy to see you and Mi-chan. Please take care of yourself and travel home safely."

My uncle drove us back. My mother had asked him to take us past the harbor so she could show me the city. We said our goodbyes as my uncle dropped us off near the church that my mother had promised to show me. My mother and uncle bowed low to each other, and he squeezed my hand kindly as he said, "Mi-chan, you are a very good girl. Please look after your mother."

I was struck at once by the pale, grand Gothic facade of Oura Catholic Church. We walked up the steps to the building, which many believe is the oldest church in Japan. It had miraculously survived the atomic blast, although it had been damaged. We looked up to see a bronze relief honoring the twenty-six Japanese martyrs who had died in Nagasaki. The church was dedicated to their memory. I gazed at the serene white marble statue of the Virgin Mary, which had been imported from France. The statue seemed to emanate tranquility and quiet courage. My mother reminded me that Nagasaki was a safe haven for Christians after the Meiji Restoration. It was at this church that many Japanese Christians sought refuge from persecution. It was a deeply spiritual and tolerant place for both Buddhists and Christians—a welcoming and safe place for pilgrims.

"This church was built by the same person who built Thomas Glover's house," my mother explained. "I will take you there. It's only a short walk from here, and it is one of my favorite walks in all of Nagasaki."

"It feels so calm here," I replied, looking at the church. "And the statue's face is so peaceful! It is a beautiful place." I went to stand beside the statue, to see what she could see. As I looked out I could glimpse the vivid azure sky, the shimmering sea like glass, and the soft green hills in the distance.

I saw a young girl with a friend. They had their backs to us, but when she turned her head, I realized that one side of her face was so damaged and melted from the atomic bomb that it was barely recognizable as human. It looked as though she were wearing a mask, with the way her eyeballs bulged out. I was so shocked that I gasped, and the girl quickly looked away when she saw my reaction. My mother put her arm around me to comfort me, and we turned to walk away slowly.

"That girl is very brave," she explained to me softly. "She, like so many others, was badly hurt by the bomb, yet she has the courage to live and look toward the future. We must respect her strength and be compassionate."

I nodded solemnly and said, "I will, Oka-chan. I was just surprised."

"I understand, Mi-chan," my mother said. "This is *mikata*, or perspective. Everything depends on how you see things. If you change your viewpoint, you will see things in a new light and gain great insight. Step back and you will see the truth."

"I'm sorry, Oka-chan," I said. "I should have thought of her feelings first."

"Please don't be sorry, Mi-chan," my mother replied. "Sometimes the truth is very different than what you see at first glance. Just remember there is always more than one way of seeing things. We must be like the birds and see the larger view. When you are too close to a situation, you can't see the truth."

The hillsides of Nagasaki had been scorched by the radiation of the bomb. So many buildings had been destroyed or irreparably damaged by the bomb, which had left its scars on the Urakami Valley and certain areas of Nagasaki. We saw torn foundations and rubble in parts of the city. Nearly a quarter of the buildings in Nagasaki had been destroyed by flames. However, the mountains that surrounded the harbor on three sides had protected the city center and the harbor itself from the full force of the blast—a blessing in disguise.

After we left the church, my mother led me on a short walk to the legendary house of Thomas Glover, the one that inspired Puccini's *Madama Butterfly*. It was my mother's favorite opera. She knew exactly where the house lay at the top of Minami-Yamate hill, and she picked up her pace in anticipation of this treasured walk through her most vivid memories. A winding, cobblestone road led us to a deserted Western-style mansion overlooking Nagasaki harbor. The view of the deep blue water reflected the late afternoon light. It was breathtaking. Thomas Glover had been a Scottish merchant and entrepreneur who helped supply the revolution with arms and war-ships that led to the Meiji Restoration. He also brought the railroad to Nagasaki, and founded a shipbuilding company that eventually became the Mitsubishi Corporation. He also established the first Japanese brewery, called Kirin.

My mother looked so happy. She seemed transformed into a young woman again as we walked around the empty and expansive grounds of the house. She was so lively and light on her feet, like a dancer. It was strange to think that she had struggled to walk just the day before. My mother was luminous with joy and seemed to dash quickly from one place to the next, as though chasing butterflies.

"See, Mi-chan, everything is just the same as I remember. Nothing has changed," she said. Tears glimmered in her eyes as she explained the history of the house and garden. She told me that this was the oldest example of Western-style wooden architecture in Japan.

The famous Glover garden was magnificent. It had an air of majestic sadness with its fragrant, colorful blooms and plants that grew seemingly deserted by humanity. Neglected though they were, with no one left to adore them anymore, the flowers continued to bloom in defiant hope—as though they knew that someday they would be admired and celebrated again; that once again this place would be full of laughter and life.

"What happened to the man who lived here and his family?" I asked.

"He married a Japanese lady and they lived here for many years," she replied. "After they passed away, their son lived here. His name was Tomisaburo Kuraba. He died during the war." She looked wistful at the recollection.

"He used to host the most wonderful parties," she said. "All sorts of people would attend. He had friends from all over the world. He even studied in America. He was involved in the Nagasaki International Club and hosted events with international delegations."

"It must have been incredible to see all those people gathered here," I said.

I imagined how full of life and parties this palatial house must have once been. The ghostly echo of laughter and music seemed to linger in the immaculate garden.

"When I was young, I spent many happy hours here in the sunshine, looking at this view and admiring the blossoms," she said. "I saw so many fashionable and cosmopolitan people gathered here."

She stared into the distance and looked deep in thought.

"The people are all gone now, just a fleeting memory like the rest of my childhood," she said softly, tears in her eyes.

When she saw the port, her eyes seemed to light up again, as though she saw something I couldn't see. It must have been her memories of the place, still so real and vivid.

"It must have been a very special place," I observed.

"Mi-chan, you're right," she replied. "Look very carefully. This is a place your mother loved. When I moved to Kumamoto, I left behind something very precious to me. I knew you would love it, too."

"I'm so glad I could see it," I told her. "I've never seen such an amazing garden before."

"Its beauty has survived even the war," she said. "It has a timelessness about it. This is a place where people dreamed and traveled. You can still feel the energy, the excitement. It lingers in the air like electricity. Can you feel it?"

She was right. I closed my eyes and imagined the majestic ships in the middle of this panoramic scene, the backdrop of autumn foliage and rolling hills, the glistening sapphire water, ladies in fine kimonos with parasols, and sailors and merchants trading fine goods from all around the world. This was a cosmopolitan center of trade, new ideas, and energy.

"Yes," I replied. "And what a view!"

"This was Japan's gateway to the world," she said. "This port city saw thousands of foreign visitors and goods coming and going. Just imagine, Mi-chan, you could find anything here: fine silk, spices, castella. When I was a student, I loved living here, but I also wanted to see the world. I dreamed of having wings to take me far away. I would sit here and look out at the harbor and the giant ships, and wondered where they were traveling to."

"It must have been so exciting to see the ships coming and going," I said.

"It was, Mi-chan. There was so much life here every moment," she said. "But my destiny was in Japan and everything was prearranged, including my marriage. I was happy to obey my parents' wishes. Remember, Mi-chan—you always have freedom in your mind. I want you to go wherever your heart takes you. The world is as boundless as your imagination."

I nodded. Here in this enchanted place, like on Hanaokayama, I felt that anything was possible.

We walked through the city and saw the famous torii at Sanno Shrine from a distance. The bomb's blast had shattered half of the torii, but one stone column and top remained among the burnt trees. Its defiant and imperfect silhouette, standing tall despite its brokenness and the surrounding devastation, seemed like a symbol of hope and courage. It reflected the resilient spirit of the city of Nagasaki and its heritage of adventure and innovation. I sensed that the city's glory would not fade. Someday there would be laughter and life in Thomas Glover's garden again, and tall ships would set forth from the harbor to seek new adventures.

Your mind is powerful, boundless,
and free like *umi*, the sea.

五

CHAPTER 5

KOKORO / HEART AND MIND

Every morning I greeted the familiar trees and plants near the water pump.

"*Ohayo, takara-san,*" I said, and beamed, remembering that my mother told me I was her treasure. I felt so wonderful and privileged to breathe the clean air deeply and feel the gentle breeze that rustled the leaves and petals of the blooms on this enchanted flower mountain. I stretched my arms toward the sky as if to touch the billowy clouds floating past. I danced up the hill and the steps back toward our little house. My feet felt light, as though they were carried effortlessly by the wind.

"Today, you are going to begin your lessons," my mother explained as she prepared our breakfast.

"Will it be like school?" I asked with curiosity. I hadn't been to school since my illness. It seemed strange to think that I should have been in a classroom but instead found myself here on this mountain high above the city. My surroundings couldn't have been more different.

"Yes, that's right, Mi-chan. You will learn the ancient wisdom of this mountain. We will begin after breakfast," she replied.

We ate a simple and small portion of root vegetables from our ration of food. My mother explained that the roots were full of nutrients from the soil, which would help me grow strong. The food was very plain, but I didn't complain since I knew how lucky we were to have this small meal.

After we finished our breakfast, my mother set up a small table as a desk. On this sat the small notebook that my mother had made for me with white rice paper sewn with thread. I loved looking at the title in exquisite calligraphy: Mimi *no Michi*, meaning "Mimi's Roadmap." I always admired my mother's flawless brushwork in the black ink title and the pink painted cherry blossoms surrounding it. This was to be my guide to our lessons on Hanaokayama. Inside, the book had my mother's writing, as well as blank pages for me to fill.

"Oka-chan, this is such a beautiful book. *Ureshii*, I'm so happy," I exclaimed.

My mother smiled and said, "Remember that these teachings will be a guide for your life. I am so happy you like the book. It's small, so you can put it in your pocket and carry it everywhere you go."

"*Arigato*, thank you, Oka-chan! I will treasure it always," I replied. I felt very important to have such a special notebook for my lessons. To me, a blank notebook was exciting because it represented unlimited possibility. Its pages were blank to fill with wisdom, like a life the chapters of which are yet unwritten.

"Today is the first day of Hanaokayama school. We must start our lessons in the proper way," my mother explained.

"First, we must thank our ancestors for this place and for your health," she said. We reflected silently for a few minutes and bowed deeply in gratitude.

"Now," she said, "let us go outside and prepare to enjoy a new day."

We stood beside the tall guardian trees that encircled our little house. "Mi-chan," my mother began, "we will start our day with very simple exercises. It is very important to fill your lungs with fresh air and stretch."

I followed her lead and breathed deeply in and out. The air was pure and filled with the sweet scent of spring: fresh grass and blossoms. Then I stretched my arms out as if to touch the sky. I felt as though the sun's warm rays were illuminating me, and I was reborn.

We wandered up toward the walking paths with the most stunning views from the mountain. The carpet of fresh grass was soft under my feet, the towering trees seemed to bow gently, and the birds chimed as we walked along the tranquil green slope.

"Next you must clear your mind through walking meditation," my mother said. "This means to focus and be aware. See only what you are looking at as you walk, and do not let your mind wander to other things. See and appreciate nature and clear your mind."

"*Hai*, yes," I said. "What should I do when other thoughts come into my mind?"

"At first, many thoughts will come to you," she told me. "But continue to walk and focus on your surroundings. Do not think, just observe and absorb all that is around you and be present in this moment. See and feel nature around you. Admire its beauty and strength, and experience it. Clear your mind of clutter and anxiety, and you will be free."

I observed the fresh smell of the grass, the glistening of dew, the subtle movements of the wispy clouds that glided subtly across the pristine sky. I watched the dark silhouettes of the birds overhead and their flight, so graceful and swift, contrasting with the stillness and solidity of the mountain. The swirling thoughts in my head slowly began to recede like waves leaving the shore and lessening in their intensity. I was now focused on my surroundings and living in the present moment. Later, I would discover that this is known as mindfulness.

"Starting today, we are going to learn about the power of your mind," she said.

This sounded very mysterious, and I was eager to hear more.

"I'm looking forward to my first lesson," I replied.

"Let's sit down, and I will teach you in the same way I learned when I was young like you. This is ancient wisdom passed down from generations," she said.

"*Hai*, yes," I said. I sat down near her on the soft grass.

"Mi-chan, you have been given a great gift," my mother said. "And it is all contained here." She pointed to my head.

"What's that?" I asked. "My head?"

"Your *mind*," she replied. "Only you can control it, and it is linked to your heart. This is what we mean by *kokoro*, the unity of mind and heart. It is the most important thing in the world."

She opened my little notebook to a page. In perfect calligraphy was written "kokoro." This was our first lesson.

"Kokoro," I repeated. My mother nodded.

"Your mind is your own limitless, empty space," she said.

"Like the sky?" I asked with wonder.

"Yes, Mi-chan, that's right," she replied. "Your mind is vast like the sky. It can be filled with dazzling ideas and dreams like stars. With a strong, clear, and united mind and heart, you can discover extraordinary things and unlock life's mysteries. With this universe in your mind and heart, you will never be lonely."

I nodded. It sounded so exciting to have my own universe. I could picture the night sky like ink, full of shooting stars glittering and disappearing.

"But our mind can become cluttered with too many thoughts and worries," she explained. "What should you do if it's too full and disorganized?"

"Clear my mind?" I suggested.

"Yes, Mi-chan," she said. "We must clear our minds. And how do we do this?"

"Look at nature," I said. "Like during our walk."

"That's right, Mi-chan," she replied. "Look at nature and truly see and experience what is before you: the sky, trees, and flowers. When you do this and fully immerse yourself in nature and in the moment, whatever else you have in your mind will disappear. Your thoughts and problems will flow away like water. Try it now as we walk. You can't be sad if you see all this beauty around you."

I thought back to the priest's comment about walking meditation. This must be what he meant. I looked closely at the curve of the sloping hills, the blades of grass glistening with dew, the wispy clouds drifting in the clear azure sky, and the vivid wildflowers that dotted the grass. I focused on my surroundings and let my thoughts flow away like water as my mother had said.

For the first time, I was seeing everything around me without any distractions—my senses were extraordinarily heightened. There was so much to see. The world was suddenly vivid, and seemingly ordinary things were astonishing and miraculous. I could see the tiny ants climbing across the grass. I noticed the way the morning light made the new grass shimmer like a sea of glass. I could hear the sound of an insect buzzing near my ear, and the rustling of the leaves and blossoms in the breeze, like a silk kimono carried by the wind. The mingled scent of the grass and flowers was everywhere. Why hadn't I noticed these things before?

"You are doing well, Mi-chan," my mother said after a long silence. As she observed me, she could see the light of recognition dawning in my eyes. "You are learning how to clear your mind. Immersing yourself in nature is one way. You can also put your thoughts in compartments like drawers to keep them tidy. Focus on the present moment and put your other thoughts away for later. You *can* control your thoughts. Do not fear them."

I nodded. In my mind, I imagined opening drawers in the sky and putting away thoughts like stars, saving them like ornaments for another occasion.

"Mi-chan, always remember that you are unique, and you should never be jealous of others," she told me. "Does the butterfly envy the birds or the trees?"

"No," I laughed. "That would be silly."

"That's right, Mi-chan. Each one has its own noble purpose," she said. "Remember that no one else in the world is like you and sees things as you do. You have special talents. Believe in yourself. You must have *jishin*, confidence. You have incredible strength and courage within you. Let your true self shine and be fearless."

I nodded, "*Hai*, yes."

"You know that your name means 'fulfillment.' What will your future be, and what dreams will you fulfill?" she asked me. "This is for you to discover as you learn how to focus your mind. Your future is like your mind—vast and full of possibilities."

"I see," I replied, thinking about what the future might hold. It seemed like a blank canvas, an unknown space that might be filled with wonderful things, like the universe in my mind.

"We constantly make decisions that shape our lives. You need to be strong to see the road ahead of you and sense what the right path is," my mother explained. "All creatures in nature face challenges. The key to survival is having a strong mind. You always have the power to make choices and keep your problems and ideas in their proper place. Just as we keep our house very neat, your mind should be free from clutter: negativity, fear, and worries."

"I understand, Oka-chan," I said. I imagined my mind being swept clean like a tatami mat.

The next morning, we walked further up Hanaokayama so we could get a different view of the city. The grass was longer there, and less contained. Bright wildflowers seemed woven into the sprawling green carpet like green, purple, and pink embroidery on silk. The earth was soft and springy beneath my feet.

"*Mikata* means 'perspective,'" she told me. "Do you know what this means?"

"Is it to do with how you see?" I ventured.

"Yes," she said. "That's right, Mi-chan. How you see things is very important. It can change everything." She drew a circle on a patch of dirt on the ground with a stick.

"If you have a problem, how should you solve it?" she asked. My mother gestured to the circle she had drawn. "Place your problem and worries in one circle and step out of it. Now look at the circle from the outside." She drew a dot outside of the circle.

"When you are too close to a problem, you can't see anything else," she explained. "But when you take a step back, you can see many ways around your challenges. Distance makes your problem seem a lot smaller and less scary. Change your perspective and you can find a solution."

I frowned in confusion.

She noticed my expression. "Let me explain, Mi-chan," she said.

"Perspective is the key to solving any problem in life. When you're too close to a situation, it's like standing in front of an enormous rock that blocks your view. You can't see what lies beyond. You need to take a step back to see the bigger picture." She gestured toward the stunning sky of pristine deep blue, the rolling hills, and the city below.

"What do you see when you look at the view from here?" she asked.

"The city," I replied. "Everything looks small from up here."

She smiled and nodded as she said, "You're right, Mi-chan. That is perspective. Taking a step back can transform how you see things. If you were standing at the base of the mountain now, what would you see?"

"Not much," I said. "I could see what is directly in front of me, but I wouldn't be able to see beyond the buildings."

"Yes, Mi-chan," she replied. "That is true. Perspective is a shift in the way you see things. You must step away from the situation you're in to see clearly."

We continued our walk, and she asked me how the view changed as we moved. What new things did I observe, and how had my perspective shifted depending upon where I was standing? It was incredible to realize how much depended on my vantage point, including the effect of the sun's rays on the city—which parts were illuminated and which were obscured by shadow.

Now I understood what she meant. What was real depended on where I was standing and how I was looking at something. I felt like I was flying from this height, and every turn brought new truths and discoveries. The flowers looked like blobs of paint from afar. Up close, they had so much intricate detail.

This is how the world must look to the hawks and the sparrows, I thought. *What was enormous to us must seem tiny from such a height*. I remembered the ants during the war. It was the same idea. Our perception of reality has everything to do with our vantage point.

"Now, I will teach you how to solve any problem in life," my mother said. "Are you ready?"

"*Hai*, yes," I nodded. We both sat down on the grass.

"How are you feeling?"

I paused thoughtfully and hesitated to speak.

"Please don't be afraid to be honest, Mi-chan. What is on your mind?" she asked.

"I'm worried," I said.

"Why?"

"I'm missing so many days of school. I'm worried about falling behind," I replied.

"What do you fear? What is the worst that could happen?" she asked. "Face your fear. We are afraid of the unknown."

"I'm afraid of failing," I said. "The worst that could happen is that my teachers would be disappointed and ask me to leave school."

"What would happen then?" my mother asked.

"I'd have to learn at home," I said.

"And what are you doing now?" she asked.

"I'm learning at home," I said, and smiled. Now I understood.

"Now are you worried?" she asked.

"No," I grinned. "The worst isn't so bad after all."

"That's right, Mi-chan," my mother said. "Our fear can stop us from living, and it takes up precious space in our mind. Once we confront it, we can see how things really are. They are never as bad as we thought. We are standing here and find we're overlooking the world rather than standing in front of a rock. Anything is possible if we believe and have courage. Challenges are merely barriers in our mind. They prevent us from making progress. We cannot see beyond these rocks in our mind. You must be like a hawk to soar beyond them and see the infinite possibility in life."

Now I understood.

"Remember when you were afraid of the dark, Mi-chan?" my mother asked.

I nodded. "I thought there were monsters in the dark."

"That's right," she said. "But then you discovered there weren't any. It was just your fear trying to trick you into believing imaginary things. This is the same. The fear is like a rock in our mind, blocking our view of the magnificent world around us and hiding the truth. Don't let it stop you from seeing how wonderful the world really is."

"I won't, Oka-chan," I said.

"This brings us to our final step: seeing paths around obstacles," my mother said. "There is always more than one way of seeing. Opportunities always exist alongside challenges."

I didn't understand. "What do you mean, Oka-chan?" I asked.

"I'm glad you tell me when you don't understand," she smiled. "Honesty is important. What I mean is that you need to see beyond each problem. Sometimes you will feel stuck, but don't give up. Just like when you were afraid of the monsters in the dark, you were brave and didn't give up."

I nodded. I was beginning to understand.

"If you were walking in the forest and suddenly your path was blocked by a boulder, what would you do?" she asked.

"I'd try to go around," I replied.

"If you couldn't go around because there was a whole wall of boulders that you couldn't climb, what would you do?"

"I'd walk in another direction and find a new path," I said.

"Exactly!" she said, delighted by my answer. "Reflect and you'll find a new path to follow. Now you see that what you feared isn't scary or hopeless after all. That is perspective. It brings you peace and clarity."

Now I understood. Fear was like a shadow that obscured parts of the valley in the distance so that they almost disappeared. A change in perspective was like a change in the angle of the sun or the spot where I was standing. Suddenly, the shadowy valley was illuminated and splendid. What once seemed hopeless and dark was now bright and full of promise. You had to persevere, so you could be in the right place to see it.

She took a round mirror from her pocket and held it up toward me. "Remember that negativity, fear, and greed are your enemies, Mi-chan," she said. "Deflect negativity like a mirror deflects light." She held up the mirror to the light to show me.

"What happens when the sunlight hits the mirror?" she asked.

"The rays bounce back," I replied.

"Exactly," she said. "You must be like a mirror. Let the negativity bounce off of you and reflect it back to its source. This is the best way to guard yourself against negative people. They are fearful. Do not let them cloud your mind with darkness. Like a shield, deflect their energy rather than absorbing it. Do you understand?"

"Yes," I said. "Negative people are full of fear and sadness. They want to make me feel the same way."

"That's very wise, Mi-chan," she said. "They will try to make you believe there is no hope and dreams are empty. But those who have hope, dreams, and love are the ones who achieve great things and change the world. The sunrise reminds us every morning that light is more powerful than darkness."

"*Hai*, yes," I said.

"Musashi-sensei said that warriors use strategy as a weapon, and you must train every day," she told me. "His first rule is 'never be dishonest.' Remember that. Always be honest and have honorable intentions. Do not let others change your behavior or your values. As he reminded us, you must see what can't be seen on the surface. Trust in your intuition. Your heart will guide you if you learn to listen to it."

At that very moment, a white butterfly flew past us, its gossamer wings translucent in the golden light.

"The spirit of our ancestors is with us," I said in wonder. I felt as though they were acknowledging the importance of these teachings and watching over me as I learned.

"That's right, Mi-chan. Remember, nothing is ever hopeless. There is always a new way of seeing and a new path to follow. Remain calm and step back. See what lies beyond," my mother said and gestured toward the horizon. "Let the light illuminate your path."

I looked toward the mountains in the distance. The vast landscape lay before me, and I felt at once dwarfed and exhilarated by the possibilities beyond. I understood what she meant. The world was so vast, but so, too, were our minds and the possibilities within us.

"What is the best way to practice these teachings, Oka-chan?" I asked.

"That's a very good question. Just like anything else, this requires tremendous practice until it becomes habit," she explained. "Take a walk and reflect in nature every day. This will help you see things in a new way."

"Walking meditation," I nodded.

"That's right, Mi-chan. Nature will always be your best friend and keep you company," she replied. "You can always turn to nature whenever you feel overwhelmed and alone. You'll see that creatures are always trying to survive. They continue to live bravely, fulfilling their destiny. Even the sparrow that loses her chick during a storm will return to her nest the following spring to raise more young. She never gives up, and she fulfills her purpose with courage and resilience."

"How are they so strong and cheerful?" I asked. "It must be difficult sometimes." I imagined the struggles of these little birds, fighting for survival in the cold winter months, huddling for shelter in the rain and constantly seeking food for their young and avoiding predators.

"They focus on what is truly important, Mi-chan," she replied. "They do not worry about money or material things as people do. They are not full of fear and greed. Creatures live simply and care for the ones they love. This is the ultimate sense of perspective. They see only what is truly important."

"I understand," I said. I had so much admiration for these brave little creatures now. I looked above at the sky and then at the grass, as I observed the swiftly moving shadows of their wings.

"They're amazing," I said. I put my arms out and ran across the grass, pretending to glide as they did.

My mother smiled as she watched me run with the wind in my hair.

"They are," she said. "I want you to be like them, Mi-chan. Fly into the light and be free."

Kokoro, unity of mind and heart, allows you
to unlock your true potential.

CHAPTER 6

YUME / DREAM

One afternoon, we were wandering around the grounds of Hana-okayama and came across a group of monks. We had just seen the tall priest and he invited us to explore the area and to visit any time. It must have been a curious sight for the monks to see my mother and I wandering around, although my mother said that the priest would have explained to them that we were staying at Hanaokayama. They had recently begun constructing a new temple.

I often imagined that I was a novice in training to become a monk. They had such discipline. I was fascinated listening to their rhythmic chanting.

"Mi-chan," my mother said, "you have been learning how to clear your mind of clutter. Now that you have learned how to remove your fears, doubts, and worries, there is so much empty space to fill."

"It's like our little house," I said. "It's so clean and bright."

"That's right, Mi-chan," she smiled. "Now we've cleared you mind to make room for *yume*, your dream."

"What is my dream?" I asked curiously.

"You can discover your dream by knowing yourself," my mother said. "What makes you happy? What do you want to achieve? Spend time reflecting and listening in silence and your heart will reveal the answers to you. Then you must focus. Your mind is strong, and if you believe and focus, anything is possible."

I listened attentively and reflected on what my dream might be. I focused purely on this. Then, in the clearness of my uncluttered mind, I saw the tall ships we had seen in Nagasaki and the magnificent view of the harbor from the pale church. I knew the answer.

"Adventure," I said. "I want to see the world!"

"You will, Mi-chan." My mother beamed at me. She knew I had her adventurous spirit. "If you focus, you will become what you dream and think."

This was an exciting discovery. I could imagine my dreams and they would become real. I thought of all the exotic places I would travel to someday. My eyes brightened as I saw these places so clearly in my mind. If I thought of them, then I might someday see them and make my dreams tangible and real.

"Wherever life's adventures take you, always remember to show *kansha* for everything you receive, not material goods but acts of kindness. Always help others in return," my mother said.

"*Hai*, yes," I replied. "Like the soldier who saved my life. I will never forget him."

"Yes, Mi-chan. That's exactly what I mean," my mother said. "Without appreciation and kindness, people would destroy themselves, others, and nature. Kindness and gratitude connect us all. We are all linked, so our actions affect one another. Remember that brave soldier. His heroic action kept you alive, and every life you touch and your good deeds have been made possible by his courage. You must never forget his kindness and sacrifice."

"I will never forget, Oka-chan. I am grateful to him every day," I said. I bowed low to show my respect for his memory.

"Believe in yourself. There is no one like you in the whole world," she replied. "I love you and I am so proud of you. He, too, knew your life was worth saving."

"*Arigato*, thank you." I bowed low.

As we walked, there was such an overwhelming sense of serenity. The trees and flowers seemed to sway in unison with the breeze. I could hear birdsong and I felt uplifted by the sweetness of the melody, which blended with the distant chanting of the monks.

"The only thing that limits us is fear. Freedom from fear gives us wings to soar." She pointed upwards toward the graceful sparrows whose dark silhouettes contrasted against the pale sky. They climbed higher and higher until they seemed like tiny specks in the distance. I watched them until they disappeared.

"What must you be like?"

"A mirror," I replied.

"Why?"

"To let the negativity and fear bounce off of me."

"That's exactly right," my mother said. "Look at those clouds moving across the sky, ceaselessly. Life is passing every moment before us, even now, just like those sparrows flying above. You never know what awaits you. Live every moment of your life with joy. Life, like everything else, has a beginning and an ending, like these magnificent cherry blossoms that are so vibrant now, but will soon fall to the ground and wither." She lifted a few fresh, creamy petals from the ground and collected them in one hand, then gathered dried, withered ones in her other hand.

"See how our view of the same thing changes over time? Nothing ever stays the same, and time does not stand still. We must treasure every precious moment. Every moment is a gift," she said.

"I will, Oka-chan," I said.

My mother and I often visited the monastery grounds and the open spaces of the mountain. We spent every day writing new notes in my book, reciting these teachings and practicing the steps to solve problems. She also taught me famous haiku poems that showed the duality of nature. I learned that everything had two sides, and that so much depended upon how we looked at things—just like the view of the valley from the top of Hanaokayama.

She recited Basho: "Every now and then / the clouds at night intercept / the view of the moon."

She also taught me about the Buddhist monk Ryokan, who wrote:

> If there is beauty, ugliness must exist.
>
> If there is right, wrong must exist.
>
> Wisdom and ignorance must coexist.
>
> You cannot separate delusion and enlightenment.

"You see, Mi-chan?" she asked. "When we acknowledge beauty, we are also admitting there is ugliness, for beauty is defined by its opposite. The same is true for joy and sadness."

I had never thought of this before. Each couldn't exist without its opposite.

"Always be yourself, and do not embrace conflict. Live in a state of peace," my mother explained. "As Ryokan said, we are constantly drifting in a world of dreams. Remain calm and let things be."

I thought of the war and all the violence, devastation, and loss that conflict and fear brought to our city. Now, Kumamoto had been transformed once again into a place of serenity. Where there had once been a circle of red flames and burning bodies, there was now grass and flowers. I promised myself that I would always promote peace, not conflict. This was my duty. The soldier had died so that I could have a future full of hope, so I could stand here among the flowers and the birds.

Every day, I recited her teachings amid the backdrop of the hills. We always began with a prayer in the morning with the rising sun. At sunset, as the flaming orb descended behind the distant hills, we ended with a blessing and thanks to all the people who had helped us. I could hear the distant, rhythmic chanting of the monks and the steady beat of their small hand drums. It was comforting to know that such faithful people gathered here loyally every day, and that I was now numbered among them. This mountain truly was a revered place of peace. The serenity flowed through this place and connected everyone and everything in an infinite loop.

"Have sunshine in your heart, a smile on your face, and a song on your lips," she would remind me. It was her mantra. She said that I could never be sad as long as I kept true to this promise. I knew she was right. Whenever I sang, I felt so full of happiness and confidence. I couldn't help but smile. I wondered how anyone could be unhappy if they were singing.

We often sang our favorite folk songs. I knew all the words by heart. I loved listening to my mother's clear voice, which the breeze seemed to carry across the mountain like birdsong.

One afternoon, we were sitting on the grass and watching the birds fly overhead. I loved to see the shadows of their silhouettes on the grass, and then look up to see a flutter of wings as they glided into the blue beyond. I wondered where they were going, and this made me think about where each of us was headed, about the great adventure that my mother said awaited me. The beyond was unknown, as vast as the ocean or as infinite as the night sky full of stars.

"Do you know what your purpose is, Oka-chan?" I asked her.

"That's a very deep question, Mi-chan," she said, smiling. "You are my *takara*, my treasure. When you were born, I promised to protect you regardless of the suffering in the world and the uncertainty of the future. This became my purpose. We don't know what the future holds for us. It is a complex, interconnected knot with many strands, the various people whose lives and moments connect with ours. I know my life is connected with yours, and it is my duty to look after you and ensure that you find happiness and strength within you."

I liked the idea of the world being connected in a mystical pattern. I imagined a complex tapestry or exquisitely embroidered kimono or even the tatami mat on our floor. Our lives are all connected and intersect in mysterious ways, like my life and the soldier's. Was this chance or part of a larger plan?

Although my mother seemed very weak and her pace had slowed considerably these days, she was very excited to teach me about life, and her eyes always twinkled with curiosity and laughter. She often asked me, "Do you understand?" She would ask questions all the time to challenge me and make me think. She knew that self-discovery was the key to knowledge, so rather than tell me the answers to everything I asked, she would help guide me to finding them myself.

My mother enjoyed telling me stories, and each one had a lesson if I were listening closely. She told me about all the animals, trees, flowers, and vegetables on the mountain, as well as the folktales about magical monkeys and rabbits. She was such a gifted storyteller; she could bring any tale to life.

Every evening after the sun set, we walked back to our little house and had a simple, hearty supper. We often spoke about the importance of appreciating each moment. She explained how quickly time passed before us.

"When we are born, we don't know what adventures are in store for us," she said. "Like history, life is full of change, both good and bad. Despite this, we can still make a difference by embracing life. We must all choose our paths wisely and appreciate that every moment is precious and fleeting."

That evening, I was helping her prepare vegetables for our dinner. She taught me how to make fresh soup stock and how to steam vegetables. I looked forward to having sweet potatoes and the fresh green vegetables we had picked. I thought how lucky we were to have enough food to eat every day. I thought about how someday we might even have rice and udon noodles again.

"How do you know what is the right path to choose?" I asked my mother. "What if you aren't sure?"

"That's a good question, Mi-chan," she replied. "Intuition is important. You must be aware of your feelings. You will find the answer if you search for it within. You are never truly alone, for you always have that inner voice and nature to guide you. Learn to listen to it."

I didn't fully appreciate what trusting my intuition meant at the time, but I gradually learned to be in tune with my feelings and trust what my mind and heart tell me when I feel unsure about a situation.

After dinner, in our cozy house illuminated by the warm glow of the lamp, I would sit at my little desk and practice writing the words *takara*, *kokoro*, *mikata*, *yume*, and *kansha* in my beautiful notebook until they were etched in my mind and upon my heart. I liked keeping track of my lessons and how much I had learned. It was gratifying to see the tangible progress I had made. Over the months we spent on Hanaokayama, the pages become filled with writing. I tried to write the characters neatly and elegantly like my mother did. Her effortlessly graceful style of writing seemed to transform every stroke into art. I was proud to show her what I had written.

"Tomorrow you will learn about meditation," she said. "You are doing so well with your lessons. I'm so proud of you. You are like the monks training at Hanaokayama."

"Thank you, Oka-chan," I said. "I'm learning so much, more than I do at school! I wish school was as fun as this."

She laughed. "Soon you will know this all by heart, and your mind will be bright and clear as the silvery moon."

As my mother reminded me, Hanaokayama has many exquisite views that have inspired thousands and provided a backdrop for immense dreams and reflection throughout the ages, from fair noblewomen and brave samurai warriors to studious monks and romantic poets. The unique serenity of the place is like an eternal spirit that lingers and imbues every being, every flower, and every blade of grass with a sense of calm and balance. It was the most extraordinary classroom and one that truly opened my mind to a world of possibilities.

Every single aspect of this place seemed to convey the ancient wisdom I was learning from my mother. Just being in this setting was inspirational. I felt free and bold, as though I could accomplish anything I put my mind to in this place. I believed my mind could even move this mountain, such was the power of this place.

I remember sitting on the lawn in the early morning light that washed over the grass, the trees, flowers, and distant city. That morning I had watched the sunrise over Hanaokayama. It was a spectacular sight, like watching the world come to life and transform into a shimmering, golden canvas as the magnificent, radiant orb of the sun rose from the darkness and brought hope to the city. It made me catch my breath as I saw the valley transform in a sparkling sea of light, and I felt so lucky to be alive and witness such an incredible sight. It reminded me of the rising sun on our national flag, and I thought of the ancient Shinto goddess of the sun, Amaterasu, radiant with her luminous beauty.

"Surround yourself with nature and clear your mind," I could hear my mother's clear voice instructing me from where she stood further afield. "Your mind is the key to your happiness. How you see and how you approach everything in life depends on how you think. Happiness is not dependent upon material things; it is a state of mind."

I was learning how to meditate, using my mother's unique form of meditation. She said it was a simple lesson I could practice every day. I closed my eyes in silent concentration and listened to her words.

"Focus on your breathing," she continued. "Breathe in and out, calmly and slowly. With each calm breath, breathe in with the wind and exhale with the trees around you. As you concentrate on your breathing, your thoughts, doubts and worries will gradually fade away. Feel them flow away like a stream of water." I thought of the water from the well being poured from the bucket.

I felt my mind becoming empty. The thoughts were disappearing from my consciousness, like a wave receding from the shore, leaving a vacuous void. There was emptiness, silence, and my breath.

"Immerse yourself in the present moment and your surroundings. Breathe deeply and observe the nature around you. Watch the clouds drifting across the sky. Remember that each moment is precious and fleeting, like every moment of your life. It is a miracle that you are alive."

I opened my eyes and watched the clouds ceaselessly moving in swirling patterns against the vivid azure sky as though I were seeing them for the first time. I heard the pure sound of birdsong like a bell chiming and calling me to prayer. I felt it echo in my heart. I sensed the breeze caressing my cheeks and observed the rustling grass. The sweet scent of cherry blossoms filled my nostrils as I breathed deeply.

I was struck by a profound sense of calm and unity with the natural world, of being attuned to all of my senses and aware of every minute movement around me. So much life surrounded me, and now I felt I was a part of the mountain's expansive spirit. With each calm breath, I felt I was breathing in with the wind and exhaling with the trees around me. We shared the same air. I could sense it. I was becoming unified with everything around me.

"Be mindful of your surroundings, be in harmony with all of nature," my mother said. I sat in perfect harmony, in peaceful silence. I had never felt such calm before.

After a long period of perfect and unbroken stillness, my mother's voice floated across the mountain: "Now, reflect and listen. Don't think. Just listen closely. Your heart will tell you your dreams. You will discover your true self."

I closed my eyes gently and listened. Adventure filled my heart and my mind. I could see a vast and undulating ocean gleaming with light. I could see a tall ship like we saw in Nagasaki.

When I opened my eyes again, I felt renewed. My mother said, "Did your heart tell you what your dreams are?"

"Yes, Oka-chan," I replied. "I would like to travel and explore the world."

"That is wonderful, Mi-chan," she said with a smile. "You were very focused then. You must continue to practice your meditation every morning. You'll grow stronger every day."

"I will, Oka-chan," I said. "I feel like I can see more now."

"I'm so proud of you, Mi-chan. You will be able to see more clearly each day. By reflecting and emptying your mind of distractions, you'll discover what gives your life meaning," she explained. "Your worries and negativity will melt away. You can accomplish anything if you focus and keep your mind clear. Even the most complex things become remarkably simple to a clear mind."

Every day I practiced meditating on the hilltop. Gradually and with practice, it became easier for me to clear my mind immediately, to let go of the rushing, chaotic thoughts and pressing anxiety. I found that I was able to focus more clearly and deeply. I could feel the tension, uncertainty, and fear melt away. I became present in every moment, aware of nature and one with it. This gave me an exhilarating sense of lightness, of freedom.

At first I needed prompting and questioning from my mother, but over time, this process of meditation became like second nature to me. I truly learned how to switch my brain from one gear to the next while avoiding any distractions or random thoughts. These swift movements became effortless as I learned to clear my mind. I found myself not dwelling on a subject, but instead changing my focus to mindfulness, like a bird changing its direction of flight. There was purity and calm like a clear pool of water in my mind, unsullied by worry.

I found the heightened awareness of the natural world surprising. I suddenly became very attuned to the changes to the landscape, the moving parts, and the natural rhythms of the world around me. What was once ordinary became extraordinary. There was beauty and wonder in every small thing, from the delicate veins on the leaves to the palest blush of the cherry blossoms in full bloom. The ceaseless motion of the clouds reminded me of how transitory life is, how quickly moments pass before our very eyes as they shift and transform and the world spins on its axis. My mother and I would sing afterwards, and I felt as though I could see and hear the blossoms transforming from creamy flowers dancing in the breeze to dry, broken petals decomposing into dust.

"I can see so much more now, Oka-chan," I said. "I can see everything moving and changing around us. It's like magic. The world is so alive. The mountain even speaks."

"That's wonderful, Mi-chan," she replied, smiling. "You can see and appreciate more now that your mind is clear. This is *jiyū*, freedom. Now you understand."

"*Hai*, yes," I said.

I wrote in my notebook about the steps for meditation. I drew a simple picture of steps leading toward a mountain, stars, and the moon. Their clear light seemed to reflect the newfound clarity of my mind, and each step took me closer to enlightenment. I had heard about *zazen*, or seated meditation practiced by monks, but I had never understood what it actually meant to empty oneself of thoughts and worries and how it helped us see much more clearly, and to discover freedom. Now I knew.

This became an integral part of my morning routine and remains so to this day, even though the backdrop for my meditation has changed. I grew to love and welcome every morning as a new miracle and a fresh beginning full of hope. I would watch the magnificent sunrise each day over Hanaokayama in awe and complete mindfulness, as though seeing it for the first time. I would sit and meditate as the world was transformed into gold and my mind became a clear pool of water reflecting the golden rays.

There is so much power in the mind, I learned. How was it possible that our minds could determine our entire outlook and change the way we perceive the world? It could. The mind is the key to everything.

I began to understand that anxiety is linked to fear and selfishness. When before I had been anxious and worrying, I was thinking of myself and was controlled by my fearful thoughts, which limited my ability to see beyond myself and my problems. When I meditated, I now emptied my mind of myself, of petty concerns, fear and vanity. I let that universe in my mind expand. I became one with something much greater than myself: nature and the whole world around me in that present moment. I found unity and serenity instead of division and conflict, and the former are far more powerful. They can liberate you from fear and unlock your true potential. I remembered my mother holding up the mirror to the sun's rays.

This freedom is what the priest must have meant that others sought here, and that he hoped we would find. I learned to empty myself and be as clear and still as a pool of water or the silvery moon.

Meditate and reflect, and your heart will
tell you your *yume*, your dream.

CHAPTER 7

MONO NO AWARE / IMPERMANENCE

One morning, after several weeks of consistent practice and concentration on my lessons, my mother said we were venturing slightly beyond Hanaokayama and the central part of the city for a special trip. I was curious but dutifully followed her without question as we left the mountain and journeyed toward an unknown destination. We walked all the way down the mountain path and then traveled beyond the city. It was a long walk, but the air was fresh and invigorating. I had that thrilling feeling of adventure into the unknown. I wondered where we were going. It seemed as though every step brought us closer to a new horizon. We had spent so much time learning our lessons on Hanaokayama that I had almost forgotten there was life beyond our enchanted little mountain.

Eventually, we found ourselves in Suizenji Jojuen, a lush garden in the outskirts of Kumamoto that was first built in the seventeenth century and completed by several generations of Hosokawa lords. The gardens were designed to replicate the fifty-three stages, or views, from the ancient Tokaido Highway between Kyoto and Edo (now Tokyo). Sadly, the Izumi Shrine, the final resting place of the Hosokawa family, had burned down in the war during the attacks on the city. There was also the Kokin-Denju-no-Ma teahouse, which had been moved here from the Imperial Palace in Kyoto, and the Nogakudo, a Noh theatre. Despite the damage from the war, the gardens were still stunningly beautiful.

The clear water in the lake was fed from a fresh natural spring underneath. My mother said this pure, special water flowed underground from Mount Aso over the course of many years and was believed to bring long life to those who drank it. The water was especially good for tea because of its purity. People believed that this is why this location was chosen.

I loved to see the brightly colored koi gliding through the water with such grace. It was exciting to see flecks of shimmering gold and vermillion suddenly appear near the glassy surface of the water and then vanish below as if by magic. This setting seemed like the ideal home for these sacred fish, surrounded by majestic green trees and hills and pure water.

"*Ma* means 'empty space' in the physical world," she explained to me. "*Ma* is found in the blank areas in paintings, the silence between words and other sounds, the gaps between the walls of a building, and the air around the landmarks in the landscape before us. Do you see it? Imagine if you were painting the scene. What would you fill with ink? What would exist in the places around this?"

I looked ahead. There was the glistening and undisturbed lake, then the green slopes and elegant pine trees above, then the sky. I imagined the dark brushstrokes. I would paint the hills and the trees, then the waterline. The rest would be blank. This was the empty space.

"Yes," I said. "The water and the sky."

"Yes, exactly," she said. "If we painted this scene on a scroll, we could paint the mountains and trees and the edge of the lake. The emptiness of the scroll would show there was sky above and water below. The white space implies this, and so the empty space is important. The beauty of the notes played on the koto impresses us, but the pauses between the notes and after a song ends are also powerful. The sound could not exist without the silence around it. Do you understand?"

"Yes," I replied. I imagined this scene painted in *sumi-e*, black ink, on the rice paper scroll in my mind. There was beauty in its stark simplicity. The picture would be incomplete without the empty space.

"There is empty space, or nothingness, in our minds," she continued. "Just like we see empty space before us in nature, we also have empty space in our minds. What do you think this means?"

"A clear mind: free from worry and fear," I said.

"Yes, Mi-chan. Like this lake. It's not muddy or mossy. It is perfectly clear and serene and reflects its surroundings. This is *mizu no kokoro*. Your mind becomes pure and calm like water. You are free from fear, anger, and selfishness. Your mind is like a still lake, reflecting the world around you," she replied.

There was silence as I reflected. For a moment, my mind became clear like the water before me and reflected the green hills, pine trees, and sky above. My mother sensed this illumination, the understanding dawning in my eyes.

"When your mind is pure and empty, what can you see?" she asked quietly.

"Everything around me," I said in wonder.

"Yes," she said. "You reflect your surroundings like this lake. You can see so much when you discover *mu*, that empty space within your mind. When you are empty of yourself, you are nothing, but you can see and sense everything. You transcend your normal existence and become free and fully aware of your surroundings. You and your environment become one. There are no barriers between the internal and external world. You become this pool of water. You are nothing, yet you are everything."

"If I am nothing, how can I be everything?" I asked.

She said, "Because you are free from emotion and anxiety. You are no longer you, Mi-chan, with your own worries and fears cluttering your mind. You are part of something much greater than yourself. Your mind is pure and you are fully present. You exist in complete harmony with nature. You are a mirror reflecting the universe."

Now I understood.

As we walked past the teahouse, my mother explained the history of the tea ceremony to me and how tea was first brought to Japan from China by Buddhist monks in the ninth century. It developed over time, and the tea ceremony became a highly cultivated art form and a spiritual ritual. She explained how a simple arrangement of wildflowers or a scroll with exquisite calligraphy would be displayed in the teahouse alcove, the *tokono-ma*, to be admired by the guests according to tradition. A simple tatami mat covered the floor.

Then we strolled past the Noh theatre. My mother taught me about the 800-year heritage of Noh, its Shinto roots, and how this form of theatrical performance was developed by Kan'ami Kiyotsugu and his son Zeami Motokiyo, who performed for the shogun in the fourteenth century. The Noh stage was simple and open on three sides, a back wall painted with a pine tree. The actors would wear masks and costumes and were accompanied by the music of flutes and drums. The actors would get dressed in the *kagami-no-ma*, or mirror room, where they would clear their minds. This emptiness would make room for their character. As they put on their masks and costumes in front of a mirror, their characters would fill the emptiness the actors had prepared within themselves. They would reflect their new character to the audience, like the mirror reflects the sun's rays. As my mother explained this, I thought of the haunting Noh mask of the horned female demon. I remember seeing one once, and it chilled my very being.

"Why does the scary mask have horns?" I asked. I shuddered at the remembrance of the mask.

"That is the *Hannya* mask, Mi-chan," she replied. "It is the mask of the female demon. She was once a woman but became a demon because of her jealousy. Where do you think her jealousy comes from?"

"Fear," I said. Now I understood why the mask was so terrifying. It was the true face of a jealous and fearful person.

"That's right," she said. "Fear, jealousy, and greed make us ugly."

I thought about this, picturing the mask clearly in my mind with its menacing horns. I vowed then never to be fearful, jealous, or greedy ever again.

"Motokiyo-san wrote many plays and essays about Noh," my mother told me. "He compared Noh to *hana*, a flower, and spoke of the perfect balance between actors and the audience and the blossoming and fading of a performance."

"Like the cherry blossoms," I said.

"That's right, Mi-chan," she said. "Each performance is unique. It is born, lives, and fades like a flower, never to be seen again."

"Is there empty space in Noh?" I asked.

"Yes," she replied. "*Ma* flows throughout Noh. The pauses between the words, music, and dancing are all important. Motokiyo-san said that what each actor doesn't do is just as interesting as what he does."

"I see," I said. As I gazed at the pine trees in the distance, I imagined the Noh actors in their masks and robes gliding on the stage, the sound of the flute and drums. It must have been a wonderful sight. I thought of the crowds that must have gathered to watch, and the perfect balance that existed between the actors and audience.

As we walked back through the gardens, I admired the stately trees and green hills as I tried to discover the fifty-three stages of the journey. There was even a small green mound representing Mount Fuji. I observed the solemn bronze statue of Lord Hosokawa Tadatoshi, who initially planned the garden, silently watching us. I thought that he must be pleased to see how the garden had developed over time and had survived even the ravages of war.

Everywhere I looked, there was empty space externally and internally. Perhaps this was why this place had been specially chosen as a location for gardens, a teahouse, shrine, and Noh theatre. It was a place where the empty space in the serene landscape reflected the emptiness in our minds that was required for true understanding and appreciation. There was a perfect balance here.

"I hope you've enjoyed our visit today. Are you ready to go home now, Mi-chan?" my mother said.

"*Hai*, yes," I said. "I have learned so much today, Oka-chan. I love the gardens and the koi."

When we returned home, I wrote *ma* in my notebook and drew the simple scene of the hills, trees, and water from memory to remind me of external and internal emptiness. Such a short and simple word at once expressed so much, and yet, so little. The characters written in black and my simple sketch were surrounded on all sides by the stark white backdrop of the page. I paused for a moment to admire the beauty of this empty space.

The next morning, the sun was rising, and its rays transformed

Hanaokayama into a beautiful and iridescent land that seemed to absorb the sun's power. The gently swaying grass was washed with pale gold and the trees' new spring leaves glittered. The mountain was radiant, and she emanated a supernatural glow.

"*Kanso* means simplicity," my mother said as we walked along the hills. "What does simplicity mean, Mi-chan?"

I thought of what she had told me about the clear pool of water in my mind.

"Getting rid of clutter," I said. "Making things clear."

"That's right, Mi-chan," she replied. "The key to happiness is to simplify your life. Look to nature to find what is truly important."

I looked up as I heard the melodious song of the birds. I felt the wind on my cheeks, and my hair danced in the breeze.

"Do the birds worry about money and impressing others?" she asked.

"No," I said. "They look after their chicks and find food."

"Exactly, Mi-chan," she said. "They care for others and their survival. Nature is simple. These creatures remind us every day that love and compassion are the most important things."

As we walked past our tall tree friends, I noticed the effect of the morning sunlight through the trees and the dancing patterns it formed on the grass beneath our feet.

"Oka-chan, look!" I said.

"It's stunning, isn't it?" she said. "That is *komorebi*, the sunlight shining through the trees."

I looked up in amazement at this magical fairyland around me as the world was changed by the dawn. My mother was right. Nature was full of simple mysteries and inspirational beauty. The light could transform everything and make the leaves shimmer as though they had been dipped in gold or embroidered on the edges with delicate thread like my mother's fine kimonos.

"Oka-chan, when I stand under these trees, I feel like I'm in a vast forest!" I said. I imagined there were hundreds of trees and how mysterious and wonderful it would be to be caught in this enchanted web of light and leaves.

"Aren't they mighty trees?" my mother asked. "The light makes them even more beautiful. We are so fortunate to be here at the exact moment to see this. Moments later and the sun might have gone behind the clouds, and we wouldn't have seen all of this."

We admired the magical light for a few more minutes in silence and awe. Then we carried on walking toward our favorite spot on the hill-top with a majestic view of the valleys below.

"*Mono no aware* is the impermanence of all things," my mother said. "Everything in life is fleeting. Like the sunlight through the trees."

"I see," I said. "We were so lucky to have this moment."

"That's right, Mi-chan," she said. "It will never happen in quite the same way again. Every moment is unique."

"I never thought of that," I said. "Every moment is special and really won't happen again."

"Yes," my mother replied. "You must appreciate every precious moment. Be fully aware and mindful every second. With the joy of this moment, there is also the sadness that it is passing before our eyes. Every second, the world is changing. Time is passing."

"I understand," I said. "Things go so quickly. Can we hold on to them?"

"Yes, Mi-chan," my mother said. "You have captured this incredible moment of the sunlight filtering through the leaves. The moment is fleeting, but the memory can last forever like a photograph in your mind."

I liked the idea of capturing these moments and putting them in a special album, like the notes I wrote in my notebook. Sometimes I worried, and that meant I was thinking of other things instead of seeing what was around me.

As though she could sense my thoughts, my mother asked, "Mi-chan, what should you do if your mind is full of clutter? You often have so many thoughts and worries. We all do at times. What would you do?"

"Look at nature," I replied. "See what is important."

"Yes," she replied. "Look around you. It is that simple. There is so much beauty and wonder around us. Be present in every moment. Absorb it. Take a photograph in your mind and capture it."

My mother put a soft red cloth on our usual rock bench so we could sit down. I loved the vivid color of the cloth because it was considered lucky. Its brightness made me feel even more cheerful.

We sat down and looked at the view of the city below coming to life, glowing with the touch of the morning sun. I could see tiny dots that I imagined were people at the base of the mountain. The clumps of trees and flowers made a colorful quilt. There were so many swirling colors beneath us. It was like watching a living painting that changed every second and readjusted focus. I could even see Mount Aso in the distance, looking mysterious and mighty, silently watching over us.

"How are you feeling, Mi-chan?" my mother asked.

"Great," I replied. "I feel so strong now and my lungs are clear. I love this fresh air."

My mother beamed. "You are fully recovered, I think," she said. "Hanaokayama has healed you. Soon you'll be able to go back to school."

"But what about our lessons?" I said, concerned. "I love being here on the mountain."

"I'm glad you have enjoyed staying here," my mother said. "But we can't stay here forever. Your school lessons are important, Mi-chan. If you want to see the world, you need to focus on your studies."

"*Hai*, yes, Oka-chan," I nodded.

"You have been an excellent pupil," she said with a smile. "You have learned so much. I'm very proud of you." She looked wistful as she gazed into the distance at the valley below and the green hills. She seemed to be hundreds of miles away.

"Are you happy, Oka-chan?" I asked. I was worried. There seemed to be a deep sadness in her eyes and suddenly there was a vast distance between us.

"I couldn't be happier than with my *takara*, my treasure," she said and hugged me. "It is *mono no aware*, the impermanence of life. You are growing up so quickly, and I know that this time, too, is passing. I treasure every moment we are together."

"Me, too," I said. "This is my favorite place in the whole world. I wish we could live here forever."

"That would be wonderful, but unfortunately that's not possible," my mother said. "We were only given permission to stay for a short time until you have recovered fully and are strong enough to return to school. We must be grateful that we have had this precious time here."

"I am," I said. "It is such a magical place."

"Perhaps we can't live here forever," my mother said. "But do you know what, Mi-chan? You can return to Hanaokayama any time you like."

"Really?" I asked.

"When you feel worried or sad, Mi-chan, just think of this place and the sunlight shining through the leaves of the tall trees and the pale blossoms floating along with the breeze," my mother said. "Just thinking of this place and revisiting it in your mind will make you feel calmer and help you clear your mind. The most wonderful things in life are simple. Memories are very powerful, too."

"I understand," I said. I nodded and absorbed the serenity of this place and the world before me.

"Now Mi-chan, let us try an experiment," my mother said. "Close your eyes."

I closed them. Suddenly there was darkness and stillness.

"Now picture the scene before you and describe it," my mother said. "See it in your mind, like a photograph or a painting you have stored in a special album."

I took a moment. "I am sitting at the highest point of Hanaokayama," I began. "I can see the sloping hills and the green valley and the city below me. There are tall trees with new leaves around us and below. The sunlight makes everything glow, but there are shadows, too, in the distance. I can see the creamy pink cherry blossoms, the swirls of green leaves, and the patches of brown. There are sparrows flying in the sky, darting and swooping. Mount Aso is in the distance, so tall and mighty," I could see it now so vividly in my mind, as though my eyes were open.

"Now open your eyes, Mi-chan," my mother said.

I opened them and before me lay that very same scene I had just described from the image in my mind.

"It was so clear," I said in amazement. "I could see it before me."

"That is wonderful, Mi-chan," my mother said. "Your mind is strong. You can return to Hanaokayama any time. It lives in your heart and in your mind. You see, no matter where you are, you just need to think of this flower mountain, and you can see this view again and be present in this moment, sitting on this rock again."

I will always remember that moment of dawning understanding, of the light that illuminates the darkness in the void. That day, I made a powerful discovery. I learned I could return to my rock on Hanaokayama any time in my mind and find this eternal sense of peace and calm. I could do this even when I was living thousands of miles away in a different country. Such was the eternal power of this place and my strong memories. My love for this place and my mother make them both infinite and eternal.

My mother was right. We could not hold on to fleeting moments forever, but we could always return to our favorite memories and be fully present in them once again. This was the power of kokoro, the unity of heart and mind. Things that were powerful were always present in our hearts and our minds, and we could recall them at any time.

The time I spent with my mother at Hanaokayama always remains in my heart and is stored in an album that is kept in a treasured drawer in my mind. This is my most precious gem, the brightly burning star that illuminates my universe and guides my path. Even now, I can close my eyes and see that expansive view before me, transformed by the sun's luminous rays, and I can hear my mother's voice. I feel free and happy. I am home.

Mono no aware, the impermanence of all things,
reminds us to enjoy every moment.

CHAPTER 8

TABI / JOURNEY

My morning meditation became second nature to me after disciplined months of practice on Hanaokayama and many inspirational dawns. At first, I needed my mother to prompt me for each step, and I had to remind myself to focus and try to ignore the distracting thoughts and worries that crowded and cluttered my mind. Eventually, I was able to remember each step and clear my mind completely without help. I learned to see the still, clear pool of water in my mind, and I became one with nature, reflecting my surroundings. I looked forward to each morning and the sense of renewal and freedom that this time of reflection provided. Since that time, this morning meditation has become an essential part of my day and remains so even in my old age. In my mind, I return to Hanaokayama every morning and find that perfect serenity on the hilltop and stretch my arms to touch the sun.

One morning, after I completed my meditation, I hurried to the water pump and again asked the flowers there if they would allow me to take them to the ohaka to decorate my ancestors' graves. My mother said there was going to be a special ceremony at the temple that day, and I was looking forward to it. She had told me that this was a very important day, but she didn't say why. It felt as though we were about to embark upon a new journey.

"*Arigato, kansha shimasu*, I appreciate your kindness," I said as I bowed low in gratitude to my blooming friends.

When I returned to the house with the flowers, the priest was deep in conversation with my mother. Suddenly they paused, and she bowed very low for a long time.

"Mi-chan, you look well," the priest said to me with a kind smile as I approached. "Are you going to the *ohaka*? It is so kind of you to take such lovely flowers to honor your ancestors. Please give my prayers to your family."

"*Arigato*, thank you," I said and bowed deeply.

My mother then walked away with him, deep in conversation. I noticed she bowed several times. I wondered what was happening. I couldn't hear what they were saying, but I didn't want to intrude on their conversation. It seemed very serious.

When she returned, she said, "Thank you for waiting, Mi-chan. We must clean up the house after the ceremony. This place has been such a wonderful home. I will always be grateful for the time we spent here."

"Are we moving?" my eyes widened in disbelief. She hadn't mentioned anything about leaving this place just yet.

"We just need to tidy up the house," she replied. She began humming softly to herself. I felt that something must be wrong. It seemed strange that she hadn't mentioned anything to me about tidying up before.

When we arrived at the ohaka, the temple priest greeted us. He touched my head, as though to bless me. Then my mother walked toward the temple with him, bowing and talking. I waited patiently for her.

"Mi-chan, let us fetch some water for the purification," she said when she returned. She looked tired. I helped her carry the bucket since she seemed to struggle with the weight of it.

"*Arigato*, thank you," she replied as she smiled gently.

"Hello, Momo-chan, you have more friends!" I greeted the familiar flowers before arranging the new wildflowers in the vases. I bowed before the final resting place of my ancestors.

After the purification ritual, we said a solemn prayer.

When we were done, my mother turned to me and said, "Mi-chan, I want you to promise your ancestors that you will remember these teachings. That you are going to be strong and will never forget the soldier's gift of courage, which lives on in you."

"*Hai*, yes," I nodded and bowed low. I recited her teachings and ended by promising always to fill my heart with sunshine, sing with joy, and smile with radiance.

"I promise I will be cheerful and strong and that I won't have fear," I said.

"*Arigato*, thank you, my *takara*," my mother said, smiling. "I am so proud of you."

There was a long and formal service with many speeches and blessings for my mother. Everyone wished her well and patted my head. I didn't understand what was happening and why this was such a special day. No one explained why we were gathered, but it seemed that we were here to honor her.

"Be a good girl and be strong, Mi-chan," one of the priests said to me before we left. I thanked him and bowed low to show respect, but I didn't understand what he meant. *Why was he telling me to be strong?*

I had noticed lately that my mother was very weak. She kept

tripping and she didn't eat much. However, she always encouraged me to eat. She explained that the protein from the food would enter my bloodstream and live in me forever, supporting me and making me stronger. I took her teachings to heart, even though I hated the taste of wild onions. It upset me that she didn't eat much, even though she always insisted I had to eat all of my food to grow strong. I decided that I would tell her tonight that I would refuse to eat if she didn't eat.

We slowly walked back to the house. My mother was too weak to take the faster route up the steep steps. We took the longer, meandering path up the gentler incline to Hanaokayama past the noble trees.

"The season is changing again, Mi-chan. Can you feel it?" she asked.

I felt something was changing. Perhaps she was right. I simply nodded and said, "Yes, it's slightly cooler now."

Her pace slowed and she seemed to be very tired.

"Why don't we stop and rest for a few minutes?" I suggested.

She smiled and agreed. We sat down on old stones by the path.

"Do you remember the story of Hanasaka Jisan?" she asked.

"Can you tell me the story again?" I asked eagerly. I never tired of hearing this famous folktale, especially the way she told it.

"Of course," she said. "Once upon a time, there was an old couple who had a dog that they loved. The dog was digging in their garden under a fig tree and found a box of gold pieces. Their neighbor took this as a sign that the dog had magical powers and so asked to borrow him. When the dog couldn't find any treasure in his garden, the mean neighbor killed the dog and told the elderly couple that the dog had died. The heartbroken couple buried their beloved pet under the fig tree in their garden. Then the dog's master dreamed that the dog told him to cut down the fig tree and carve it to make a mortar. He did exactly that. When he filled the mortar with rice, the rice turned into gold. The jealous neighbor borrowed the mortar, but when he used it, the rice turned into smelly berries. Furious, the neighbor burned the mortar. The dog appeared in another dream and told his master to take the ashes from the mortar and sprinkle them on cherry trees."

My mother stopped here, "Do you remember what happens next?"

"The cherry trees bloomed and the *daimyo*, the lord, admired them and gave the old couple gifts," I said.

"That's right, Mi-chan. And can you guess what the neighbor did?"

"He sprinkled the ashes on his trees," I said.

"He did," my mother said. "But the ashes blew into the daimyo's eyes, and he sent the wicked man to prison. The old couple lived very comfortably for the rest of their lives thanks to their dog, who loved them and watched over them even after he was gone. Because of him, we can all admire these beautiful, magical blossoms."

"I love that story," I said. "I'm so glad he shared the blossoms with everyone!"

"Are you ready to go home, Mi-chan?" my mother asked, smiling.

"*Hai*, yes!" I replied happily. I held my mother's hand and we walked slowly back up the little flower mountain.

When we had returned home, I helped her sweep the tatami mat clean and tidy up the kitchen.

"Your brother is coming for dinner this evening," she said. "It will be good to have our family together again."

That evening, my brother, mother, and I gathered at our cozy little house on Hanaokayama for a family supper. As was our custom, I was served first since I was the youngest, and then my brother ate. My mother didn't. I asked her why she wasn't eating.

"I'm not hungry, Mi-chan," she said. "But thank you for asking. It's been a busy day."

I didn't dare protest as I had promised myself I would. She looked content, so I said nothing.

Silence permeated the house after dinner, and my mother and brother seemed unusually solemn. The atmosphere seemed tense. I thought perhaps my mother and brother had quarreled while I was helping to prepare our dinner. I asked my mother if we could go for a walk. I knew it would be more peaceful amid this serene and majestic setting.

"Let us look at the stars, Oka-chan. The sky is so clear," I said.

My mother smiled and told my brother that she was going to go for a walk with me. He simply nodded and did not seem eager to join us.

We went to our usual spot where she had taught me so many lessons. My mother laid the red cloth on our stone bench, and we both sat down overlooking the city with its twinkling lights below and the shimmering stars above. I thought how incredible it was that the same view now looked so different. There was such a contrast between the brilliant, fresh light of dawn and the pale, ethereal flicker of the stars and moon and the darkened city below. Whereas the world had been burnished in gold in the morning, the valley was now dipped in pale and ghostly silver. There was an otherworldly sheen cast over the distant hills and the valley below, and there was a profound hush as though everyone and everything were asleep or enchanted like in a fairytale.

"Oka-chan, please sing a song for me," I asked her.

She sang "Sakura." Her magical voice calmed me, seeming to fill the night sky like the chanting of the monks at sunset, as though it were now part of the mountain's song, blending with the ghostly melodies sung here thousands of years ago. I imagined that the stars were listening to her song, and they twinkled in appreciation, like tinkling bells chiming in unison with her silvery voice.

"Thank you for being my *takara*, Mi-chan," my mother told me. "*Ganbarinasai*, be the very best you can be and be happy. Always believe in your dreams and have courage during this *tabi*, journey of life."

"Please promise me this, Mi-chan," she said. "Promise me you will be happy and strong, always."

I looked up at her. She looked very serious, so I knew this was important to her. She extended her pinky finger to me, to make an unbreakable promise.

"I promise, Oka-chan," I replied, linking my finger with hers to accept the promise. "I will always be happy and strong."

"*Arigato*, thank you. I am so proud of you and love you, Mi-chan. Never forget that," she said and embraced me. "I have enjoyed every moment we have spent here on Hanaokayama."

"I love you, too, Oka-chan," I said. "This is my favorite place in the world. I will always keep it in my heart."

"I will, too," she replied. "Remember you can return here any time you want—in your mind."

"*Hai*, yes, Oka-chan," I replied. "I won't forget."

That evening, I slept soundly on the tatami, thinking what a strange and mysterious day it had been. It seemed like one chapter was ending and that change was imminent. I wondered what the future would hold for us.

The next morning, I woke up early and wandered outside to see the sunrise. I wanted to start the day with my morning meditation to clear my mind. I couldn't find my mother, and I wondered where she was.

"Mi-chan, *isoide*, hurry. We must go," my brother said to me when he saw me.

"What's wrong?" I sensed something wasn't right. My brother looked so severe.

"Oka-chan is at the hospital."

"Why?" I cried. "What's happened?"

"She is very sick," he said. "You were the only one who didn't know, but she has cancer. She is in the final stage of illness, and there is nothing we can do."

I felt like I had been struck down. My mind was clouding over with darkness, my body was trembling and my eyes were blurred by a flood of hot tears. This couldn't be true. My mother was so full of life and joy. It had to be a lie. I tried to open my mouth to speak, but I was in complete shock. There was no sound.

"She knew she didn't have much time left. You are too young to understand, Mi-chan," my brother said calmly, trying to be kind. "Mother made me promise to spare you pain. You never knew your father and now you are losing your mother. Hurry, there's very little time. You have to say goodbye to her."

"No!" I cried, my voice suddenly emerging and rising. "This can't be happening. This isn't true!" I screamed. I was shaking uncontrollably just as I had done during the war.

In the vast sky, where the night before there had been glistening stars, there was now pouring rain. I didn't understand what was happening. I remembered that my mother told me that spirits travel to heaven on a boat and require rain for a safe journey. Does this mean she is going to heaven now? I refused to believe that. She *had* to be well. I needed to see her immediately.

"Please wait for me, Oka-chan. I want to see you and talk to you," I whispered. "This can't be true." I remembered how weak she had been and how she hadn't eaten any food lately. *Was it possible that she knew she was dying?*

I don't even remember the journey to the hospital. I was in such a state of shock and kept feeling dizzy and sick as though I were going to faint at any moment. When we arrived, the doctors greeted us with grave faces and deep bows. They were talking with my brother, and they asked me to sit and wait nearby.

I could hear fragments of conversation. I heard one of the doctors say that they performed an operation on my mother, but it was unsuccessful and she was fading quickly. They said they had moved her to a room where we could all say farewell. When I heard this, I started sobbing and shaking uncontrollably. A nurse tried to comfort me, but I was inconsolable.

"Mi-chan," my brother said solemnly, "it is time to say goodbye to Oka-chan. Be brave."

One of the doctors opened the door to her room, and I saw my mother wrapped in a white sheet lying on a bed in an austere room with white walls. It all seemed cold and unreal, like a strange dream. Her eyes were closed and she seemed to be asleep. I touched her. She was still warm.

"Oka-chan, mommy, why didn't you tell me you were sick?" I cried, before dissolving into panic. "I am so sorry. I should have given you my food so you would be strong. Please don't go, please take me with you. I need you! Please don't go. Why are you going without me? You said you will be with me always, but they say you are going to heaven. Please don't leave me alone. Come back! Please come back!"

Burning tears streamed down my cheeks and I was convulsed with sobs. I squeezed her hand and refused to let go. As long as I could see her, I knew she was still with me and they couldn't take her from me.

I don't know how long I held my mother's hand before I fainted. The next thing I knew, my brother was gently nudging me. He told me we had to say goodbye and leave. He helped pull me up and walked me to the door. I turned around and saw my mother for the last time ever, lying on her hospital bed, completely lifeless now with her eyes closed and her body draped in white. She looked so small and peaceful, freed from the agony of her earthly suffering. Now cold but no longer in pain.

I wept bitterly and cried, "Oka-chan, please come back!" I tried to run back into the room to hug her, but my brother gently but firmly led me away and told me it was time to go home. I saw the door closing behind us, and then my mother was gone forever.

I defiantly ran ahead of my brother down the hallway. I needed to be alone. Through the bleary and fogged windows, I saw the driving rain was slowing down. I knew this meant her spirit was already on its way to heaven in its boat, carried along the water like the tall ships in the harbor at Nagasaki. I said a silent prayer for her safe journey to the Pure Land and bowed. I said to myself, *She will be back. She has never left me alone before. She will return.*

That day, I moved out of Hanaokayama forever and went to stay with my brother. Seeing the little house I shared with my mother, now empty and lifeless without her and the tatami mat so clean and bare, made my heart ache. It was no longer a warm home, for the light at its hearth had been extinguished forever. It was merely a shell; its very heart was gone. Even my tree and flower friends could not comfort me. I couldn't bear to look at them as we departed for the last time. I held on to my dilapidated little bag with my remaining possessions, clutching my treasured book she had made for me, and my little doll. Every place on that mountain was imbued with her memories and spirit. Now the place seemed cold and uninviting, devoid of her presence, familiar yet strangely altered and alien. It seemed wrong to be there without her, and the very sight of it was indescribably painful to me.

Once I was at home with my brother, he explained that my mother had been preparing me for life alone, teaching me to be strong and to have dreams and courage. That is why she had wanted to teach me on Hanaokayama and make the most of her limited time left on earth. I learned that everyone in our lives except me knew her life was coming to an end, and that her dying wish was to guide me in preparation for my journey into the future without her. We had been granted permission to stay at Hanaokayama since everyone knew I was recovering from a serious illness, and that I would only have a few more months to spend with my mother before her cancer spread. This was her dying wish: to spend time alone with me on the mountain before her life ended.

I wondered why she had told everyone except me that she was dying. It was such a shock. I couldn't believe she would keep the truth from me for all this time. How could I have been so blind and selfish and not seen that something was wrong? Why couldn't I have saved her? I felt I had failed her.

My brother tried to comfort me. He tried to make me understand that it wasn't my fault.

"Don't you see, Mi-chan?" he said. "She wanted you to be strong and happy. That is why she taught you the lessons on the mountain, and why she didn't tell you she was dying. You must remember her words and have courage. She loved you so much, and she wanted you to live and be happy. You must do that for her sake."

He found the little notebook my mother had made for me and my beloved doll and placed them gently into my hands. I clung to these treasured objects. My mother had made them for me, and now they were all I had left of her. Her great and benevolent presence was reduced to a few scattered objects. I looked at her graceful writing and thought that she would never write again. She would never sing again. I would never hear her voice again. The permanence of her death and the reality of our separation suddenly confronted me. She was gone forever.

That evening and for many more painful nights to follow, I sat alone outside the house in the rain and watched the stars glimmering in the vast night sky above me. I couldn't believe it was only the night before that we had been so happy watching the stars together and singing her favorite song at the top of Hanaokayama. I thought of what she had said about *mono no aware*, the impermanence of things.

It had seemed strangely prophetic. But she had known that her time on earth was ending.

How could life be so fleeting and delicate? It seemed unreal that one moment you could be with someone and the next moment they could vanish forever. I thought of the soldier who had died instantly before me. Truly, life was as fragile and evanescent as a blossom. The breeze had simply carried her away.

As I sat on the wooden steps, I could feel the cold rain dripping on my face, hair, and clothes, and the hot tears streaming down my swollen eyes and cheeks, but I didn't care. Nothing mattered anymore. Menacing storm clouds gathered and the moon's silvery light and the sparkling stars were obscured by their darkness. A flicker of ghostly light peeked behind the clouds, and then everything was completely black like ink, as though there had never been any light in the world. I had never felt so utterly alone and hopeless, not even during the war. I couldn't even see the tiny ants now. There was no one. I suddenly remembered my mother's words and my promise. I tried to sing and be brave and strong. I had made an unbreakable promise to her.

My voice broke and I collapsed on the ground in tears, which fell silently like the rain around me in the darkness. My face was covered in water. I felt weak and ashamed. I had promised her I would be brave and strong and happy, and now I didn't even have the strength to stand or to face myself.

Why had she left me here alone without even the faintest glimmer of hope or a single star to light my path? Even the darkest and most horrific days of the war were bearable as long as I knew I was by her side and she would protect me. Our little home on Hanaokayama had been so full of love and light. She always talked excitedly about the future and what adventures were in store for me. She never told me she wouldn't be sharing that future with me, even though she must have known the truth in her heart. I thought of the times she had seemed wistful, and I had not known why.

It occurred to me suddenly that her spirit had been transformed into a cherry blossom floating with the breeze. I could see the pearlescent blossom carried along the wind across Hanaokayama, drifting and then falling freely toward the green and golden valley below—bathed in liquid gold. It seemed fitting to think of my mother as a flower, so graceful and light, and it comforted me to think of her spirit being free to fly like a sparrow above the hills without any pain. I remembered the story of Hanasaka Jisan. There must be a reason why she told me that story again the day before she died. Perhaps she was trying to tell me that she was still watching over me and protecting me, even now.

Always believe in your dreams and have courage
during this *tabi*, journey, of life.

CHAPTER 9

MA / EMPTINESS

A t first it was too painful to see my beloved Hanaokayama without the presence of my mother, but I soon felt compelled to return. After all, it was the place I treasured the most and which was a constant reminder of her love and the joyful time we spent together. I still had faith that she would return. I was convinced that she would choose Hanaokayama as her destination, since it was our true home.

Every day after school, I would climb the familiar stone steps to the top of Hanaokayama. I needed to see my family and the landscape that cheered my heart and renewed my spirit. I said hello to my tree friends and they waved back to me in the breeze. I admired our little house, which now stood empty, used only for visitors and pilgrims seeking a quiet place to meditate. I didn't mind so much now that no one else was living there, and I could still visit and slide the shoji screen open to see the clean tatami mat and remember where we had eaten our dinner every evening.

I walked down the hillside and greeted the familiar wildflowers gathered around the water pump with their clusters of pink, purple, and verdant green and sat on the worn stone bench where I had sat with my mother. I felt like she might call my name at any moment, and I wanted to be ready for her arrival at this enchanted mountain. Every day, I waited patiently, alert to any sounds or signs of her imminent appearance. I visited all the familiar sights and places where she had taught me her wisdom. None of the familiar landscape had changed. I found this reassuring.

One day, the familiar priest walked past where I sat on the mountain. He was wearing a dark kimono and looked very dignified and stately. He stopped when he saw me, smiled warmly, and gave me a reassuring pat on my head just like old times.

"It's lovely to see you here, Mi-chan. Please come visit any time you would like, and I will say a prayer for your mother," he said kindly and bowed.

"*Arigato gozaimasu*, thank you," I said and bowed deeply as my mother had done before.

"Are you doing well? Go look at the *torii* and sit in the gardens," he urged me. "This would make your mother very happy. She loved this place. Her spirit is present. You can sense it."

"I'm very well, thank you," I replied. "I will. I love Hanaokayama, too."

I bowed low and smiled, pretending to be happy since I had promised my mother I would be strong and cheerful. I wondered at his words. *Was my mother's spirit really here? Why couldn't I see her or communicate with her?* I really wanted to ask him so many questions, but I was worried he might think I was being silly or fanciful.

Every day after school, I carried a special picnic for my mother, which I packed at home in our kitchen in a small bento box with little compartments. I wrapped the box in a special embroidered cloth and placed it carefully in my school satchel. I dutifully went to the same place where she had taught me overlooking the city. I carefully laid the red cloth on the rock like she did that final evening before she left us, and I neatly set out her food for her. She had taught me that presentation and aesthetics are just as important as taste and culinary skill, so I was meticulous in arranging her food. I also remembered that she had said that we must admire the food before we eat it since so much effort had gone into the preparation and presentation.

"Oka-chan, mommy," I told her, "today for lunch we have a little fish, spinach and pickles, but still not much rice, although at least we have enough for *onigiri*, a rice ball. I get up early every morning and cook at our house now, and I have learned to make all of our usual dishes. I saved this food to share with you. *Oishii*, isn't it delicious? A little bird is joining us now. I think she wants to be our guest."

A brown sparrow hopped nearby on the rock and looked at me with inquisitive dark eyes. I smiled and gave her a few crumbs. She pecked at them gratefully, and I thought of the little ants we had protected during the war. I wondered where their descendants were now. They must be living peacefully in the valley somewhere below.

"Oka-chan, when are you coming home?" I asked. "Everybody says you went to heaven, but where is heaven? Why can't you come home? I look up at the sky at night, and I see the same stars I saw with you. I can't see you, though. Can you see me?"

The long grass gently touched my hair, and the sweet scent of wildflowers was carried on the breeze. White puffy clouds floated lazily over my head. The bright sun warmed my skin and brought with it a sense of peaceful calm. Here my loneliness seemed far away. I felt sure my mother would be coming back from her long journey. I looked at the sky above and remembered ma, the empty space in the gardens and the white space on the rice paper. There was infinite empty space above like the universe in my mind, and around me there was emptiness between all objects. I found it soothing to contemplate this emptiness in silence.

I practiced my meditation like she had taught me, and I was mindful of my surroundings. Being in this place made me feel like I had returned to my lessons. I could hear the faithful monks chanting in the background, and I meditated silently with them until I was one with them and the birds singing in the distance.

I told her stories just like she had taught me. I made up lots of stories about the birds, the flowers, and the trees. I also read my well-worn book of fairytales over and over again to remind me of all the exciting and colorful stories she had told me. I re-read the story of Kaguya-hime, Princess Kaguya, so many times. I wept when she had to leave behind her parents to return to the moon in her chariot, which disappeared into the sky with the breaking of the dawn. I imagined I could see it disappearing into the clouds above me. Now I truly knew the pain of loss and parting with loved ones, so the story was even more poignant. I wondered if my mother had returned to the moon like Princess Kaguya. Perhaps that was why she could see me but I couldn't see her.

I also loved the cheerful and incredible Buddhist folk story of Daietsu, who was known as the straw millionaire. Daietsu, a poor peasant, prayed to Kannon, the goddess of mercy, for help. He heard her voice tell him to take the first thing he found with him on a journey leading west. After leaving the temple, he immediately fell to the ground and found a piece of straw. He took the straw and tied a horsefly to it.

As he walked down the road, Daietsu met an exasperated mother with a crying child, and he gave the straw with the horsefly to the child for comfort. The grateful mother gave him oranges. Later, he met a beautiful young woman who was thirsty, and he gave her the oranges out of compassion to quench her thirst. She thanked him by giving him an exquisite piece of red silk. He continued on his path and met a samurai warrior, who asked for the silk and offered him a sick horse in return. Daietsu obligingly took the horse and cared for it, nursing it back to health.

Further down the road, Daietsu met an elderly rich man who admired his horse and invited him to have dinner at his house. When Daietsu arrived at the man's impressive house, he met the millionaire's daughter, whom he recognized as the young woman he gave the oranges to during his journey. The millionaire was so struck by this remarkable coincidence that he took it to be an auspicious sign and insisted that Daietsu marry his daughter. Daietsu married her and lived happily ever after as the straw millionaire, the man whose fortune had been transformed by a piece of straw.

My mother said that this story demonstrates that anything is possible if we have faith and don't give up on our dreams throughout our journey of life. I thought about it, and decided that I wouldn't lose faith, and would keep waiting for my mother to return.

Although I always enjoyed my daily visits to my beloved little mountain, I became discouraged after many months of waiting. Every day, I saved my food and took a picnic for her at Hanaokayama. Every night, I waited for her return on the steps in front of our house, but she didn't come home. I kept looking up at the sky, watching and waiting, as if for a special sign in the moon or the stars. Something had to happen soon. I believed so strongly that something would, but there was no change at all. The days came and went. Time and seasons passed, but still there was emptiness, silence, and solitude.

In the evening, I would sit on the porch steps outside our house and sing softly to myself as I waited.

"Mi-chan, please come inside the house. It's getting dark. You'll catch a cold," my brother pleaded.

"No, I want to stay here, I don't want to see anyone, except Oka-chan. I know she is coming back to see me," I replied.

He shook his head, despairing at my stubbornness and impossible hope, and returned to the house, leaving me to my silent vigil. I would continue to sit outside in the dark, keeping watch patiently in silence for hours. Sometimes I could hear the chirping of the crickets, and I knew that at least I was not entirely alone.

On some days, I would walk to the temple where my mother's ashes were buried in the shadow of the tall pine trees. I remained outside, unable to enter, because I had promised my mother at this very place that I would be brave and cheerful. I sat next to the gate on a cold rock, my face covered with tears. I felt ashamed that I couldn't keep my promise to her or visit my ancestors as I had once done with her. I thought of Momo-chan, the pink flowers, and I said a silent prayer for my mother and our ancestors and asked for forgiveness.

Then I would wander up the steps to our favorite spot at the very top of Hanaokayama and sit on our rock seat overlooking the valley below, imagining I was a hawk at the summit of a mountain. Everything looked so small and insignificant down below, and the valley and hills were swathes of green, gold, and gray.

I would sit there and open my treasured possession: a letter from my mother in her unmistakable, flowing script. She had left it for me with my brother to read after she was gone. I remember the day he gave me that precious letter. It was several days after she had died, when he felt I would be in a calmer state of mind to read it and begin to understand why she had not told me she was dying. They were her final words to me and proof that she knew her days were soon coming to an end. The letter also showed that even amid her terrible pain and suffering, she was always thinking of my feelings and wanted to help reassure me of her love.

This letter was my only comfort, and I kept it safely folded in my notebook. I had read it so many times that I could recite it from memory, and the thin rice paper was worn and wrinkled like an ancient scroll. I opened it delicately so as not to tear the precious paper.

Dearest Mi-chan,

By the time you read this, I will be traveling to heaven to join your father. I have asked your brother to look after you. Please obey him. Remember your promise to me to be happy and strong. Hold on to your dreams and challenge life without fear, no matter what hardships you face.

When I look down upon you, I want to see your smile, not your tears. More than anything, I want you to be happy. Remember: when you look up at the stars, Mommy will be looking back at you proudly.

I will always be with you, my takara. Be free and fearless.

With all my love,

Mommy

As I read her familiar words, I could hear her gentle voice saying them, and I could see her kind face. My body shook, racked and aching with my uncontrollable sobbing and a deep pain in my heart that would not subside. More than anything else in the world, I wanted to see her and speak to her. I fell to the ground, weeping desperately, without hope.

I refused to accept my mother's death. I could not believe that she would ever leave me when she promised me that she loved me so much and would always be with me. If she was looking down upon me, why couldn't I see her? I raised my eyes to the heavens and searched desperately for something. All I could see above me was infinite emptiness—empty space that seemed to reflect the emptiness in my heart and spirit. *Why couldn't she at least send me a sign to show me she was there and looking after me? Did she really mean it when she said she could see me? Where was she?*

At home, I mourned my mother's death alone in silence. I continued to wait outside for hours hoping to see her frail figure appear. I kept my nighttime vigil devotedly, even in the rain. I would sing the songs she taught me and hoped I might suddenly hear her voice singing along with me. The songs comforted me, since they were a reminder of the time we spent together and the simple joy of welcoming springtime and new beginnings. She said I could never be unhappy when I was singing, yet I felt a deep sorrow. The long shadow it cast seemed to obscure any hope.

When I was very low and miserable, I sang "Itsuki no Komoriuta" also known as the Kumamoto lullaby, since it was a local folksong about a poor, lonely nursemaid serving a noble family and missing her family. My mother used to sing it to me, and its melancholy, haunting melody and words somehow matched my mood and conveyed my suffering in words that I could not express myself. It also seemed to remind me that I was not alone in my loneliness and suffering.

After several months had passed, my brother began to grow impatient with me. He felt I was being childish and self-indulgent in my grief and steadfastly refusing to accept the reality of our mother's death. One night after I had cooked dinner and was sitting alone with my thoughts morosely, he confronted me.

"Mother is dead! Don't you understand, Mi-chan? She isn't coming back. It's time to accept it. You are the daughter of samurai. You must be strong," he said, his piercing, dark eyes flashing at me with annoyance.

I backed into the corner of our small living room defiantly, trying to put as much distance between us as possible and returning his gaze with a cold, haughty stare. Summoning all the courage I possessed, I held back my anger and tears. He didn't understand, and I didn't want him to see me break down like a petulant, weak child. He didn't believe Oka-chan would return, but I knew she would. She said she would always be with me and to have courage. I had faith that she wouldn't leave me forever like this, especially when she must know that I was in such pain and had no one to turn to for friendship. My brother was stern and reserved.

"I am strong. I am my mother's daughter," I said quietly, with as much dignity as I could muster.

He suddenly seemed to feel badly about his impatience and his annoyed expression softened into one of deep pity and remorse.

"I'm sorry," he said. "Sometimes I forget that you are very young. It will take time for you to accept what has happened. It has come as such a shock since you didn't know Mother was ill. I was prepared, but you weren't, Mi-chan. Forgive me."

"I'm fine. You don't need to feel sorry for me," I replied coldly and ran outside.

I knew he meant well, but I resented his patronizing tone. I didn't want his pity, and I was convinced he didn't even begin to understand the depth of pain and inconsolable sorrow I felt. He thought I was being immature. He expected me to recover, to act as though everything was fine and normal again, but it was impossible. How could he understand that I felt that I could never be happy again and that the kindest and most generous person in the world had disappeared forever?

I sought solace in nature and was able to hold back my tears until I was outdoors and out of sight. I didn't want anyone to see me crying. I just wanted silence and solitude so I could remember my mother in peace and honor her memory.

I spent lonely hours escaping the company of others and my grief in monotonous housework, cooking, and cleaning. I didn't want to spend time with others, laughing and pretending I was happy, yet I couldn't tell anyone how I really felt. I had to respect my brother's wishes that I accept this loss silently and with dignity. This was the Japanese way. We were not expected to show emotion, especially in front of others.

But my mind was always free. My thoughts belonged to me, and I knew this universe was as safe and limitless as my mother had promised. I enjoyed getting up very early every morning to see the splendor of the sunrise and to complete my chores in peaceful silence while the world was asleep. The house and garden were wonderfully still, and I relished the time to meditate and reflect. It reminded me of all those happy and illuminating mornings of meditation on Hanaokayama as I saw the mountain and the valley below bathed in mellow light and my mind became clear like a pool of water as the sun rose. I would raise my arms to the sky and stretch as if to touch the sun. I reminded myself that every day was a new beginning. My mother had taught me about the power of light and hope to dispel darkness and fear.

I clung desperately to every precious memory of my mother, escaping to Hanaokayama whenever possible. I went there in the daytime after school since I wasn't allowed to walk alone at night. When I couldn't go to the mountain, I remembered my mother's words and revisited my treasured memories of this place in my mind. I could close my eyes and return to the mountain any time, recalling every detail of the landscape and its essence. For a short time, I felt happy and tranquil again, living in my treasured memories and returning to that sacred place that was so real to me and resonant with her spirit.

I existed in my lonely world for a long time, isolated from others and immersing myself in nature to find solace for my pain and loneliness. My only happiness was my daily picnic on the hillside. Pretending my mother was present, I would unpack my lunch meticulously and arrange rice balls, flowers, and candy across from me in my mother's imaginary place. I was proud that we now had better food to eat and could indulge in a few small luxuries like candy, which I saved for her.

"You would be proud of how much I have learned over the past few months," I explained to her. "I do all the cooking and cleaning now. And look at this candy and cake I saved for you. These are your favorite. Isn't it amazing that we can have these again now that the war is over?"

My mother had loved all sweet things, including cake, sweet mochi, and candy. These were so scarce after the war, but she often told me how she had enjoyed such delicacies when she was growing up in Nagasaki. Her father, my grandfather, was a wealthy merchant who owned a confectionary company. Sweet things like these were plentiful in her youth.

I read through the well-worn pages of my beloved little notebook, remembering our lessons about takara, kansha, mikata, yume, and ma and writing the characters diligently in my book again to remember them. My calligraphy was improving. I practiced the disciplined brushstrokes and copied my mother's flawless examples. I remembered that I had never seen her write with a pen. She only wrote with a sable brush dipped in ink. She would grind a traditional ink stick, which was made of soot and glue, on a slate inkwell filled with a small amount of water to make fresh *sumi*, ink, and paint on a fine roll of rice paper atop a piece of felt, which would absorb any excess water. Now I wanted to do the same to remember her. I also started painting with watercolors and ink as she had done. I practiced painting cherry blossoms, bamboo stalks, leaves, and sparrows.

I would meditate every morning to clear my mind and talk to the trees, flowers, and birds in the wild landscape surrounding me. They were my only friends, but I remembered that my mother had said I would never be alone, because nature would always be my faithful friend. I felt that the creatures surrounding me could understand me in a profound way that people couldn't. We were bound by the same sacred essence that connected us all, and it seemed that words were unnecessary in the natural world. We could exist happily in companionable silence and contemplate both the interconnectedness and the emptiness around us. Even the empty space was connected with objects by kami. The perfect harmony of the universe as it existed on Hanaokayama brought me solace and comfort during these difficult days when loneliness and pain ravaged my heart.

My mother's spirit seemed to flow through Hanaokayama, joining with the eternal spirit of the mountain itself. Being here seemed to bring her back in some form, and I felt her spirit was all around me, just as the priest had said to me. She was present somehow. Like Nagasaki, it was a place she loved, so it was now indescribably precious to me. The memories we shared echoed in the hills like the birdsong, and I could almost hear her silvery voice blending with the familiar chanting of the monks resonating throughout the hills. Those precious lessons were stored lovingly in the album of my mind.

I remembered all the carefree times we had spent here, surrounded by the enchanting scent of the cherry blossoms and the pure sound of birdsong carried along by the spring breeze. The mountain's face, though it changed with the seasons, was always serene, and she smiled benevolently upon me and the creatures that surrounded me. I felt that she watched over me with compassion and sensed how lonely I was, solely comforted by my memories. I lived isolated in the past for so many months, clinging to that album in my mind and imagining my mother was still present. I spoke to her every day and sat alone on this little mountain, yet somehow I didn't feel alone.

"Oka-chan, mommy, I love spending time with you," I said, and spread my arms as if to hug the air itself.

I wished she could respond or send a sign to show me she was present, but there was simply silence and emptiness to greet me. I would cry for hours until I felt I had no more tears left to cry. The tears flowed endlessly and my eyes and cheeks were red and swollen, but I didn't care. I was alone, and I wasn't ashamed of my grief. I needed to cry. I felt I had bottled up my pain and tears, since I couldn't express my emotions at home.

I would stay on Hanaokayama until twilight arrived and the sky became a deep lilac blanket woven with striking ribbons of orange and gray. It was a stunning sight. There was a tremendous hush that settled upon the mountain and the valley below as the fiery sun sank toward the horizon. When I began to see the sparkling stars emerging in the distance, I recalled that final evening and how happy we had been singing together. I remembered my unbreakable promise to her. I couldn't disappoint her or the old soldier who had sacrificed his life to save mine. I wiped away my tears and tried to smile as I had promised her.

"I promise, Oka-chan, I will be happy and strong," I said as I looked at the stars. "Can you see that I'm smiling?"

Reluctantly, I stood up and slowly walked back home. It was time to go, since my brother told me never to walk alone in the evening, and my mother said to obey and respect him.

Find clarity in *ma*, emptiness. Empty your
mind and immerse yourself in nature.

CHAPTER 10

KIBO / HOPE

On the third anniversary of my mother's death, I climbed the familiar stone path up to Hanaokayama carrying special food for her birthday. Buddhists believe the day someone dies marks a new birthday. I made sure everything I prepared was perfect to honor her memory.

"Happy birthday, Oka-chan. I can't believe it has been three years," I said.

"*Konnichiwa*," I suddenly heard an unfamiliar voice say, much to my shock.

I turned in disbelief to find a tall, elegantly dressed, gray-haired woman. She wore a dark blue suit and a starched white blouse. She spoke perfect Japanese, but she looked European with her fair skin and light eyes.

"May I sit next to you?" she asked. Her voice was gentle and calm.

I was so shocked at this unexpected visitor that I fell silent.

"My name is Miss Akard. I am the headmistress at Kyushu Jogakuin, a preparatory school for girls." She seated herself beside me although I said nothing in reply. "Do you visit Hanaokayama often? I come here frequently to enjoy the beauty of this place."

I felt she was an interloper. She didn't belong here. Miss Akard sat near the food I had set out for my mother's special birthday lunch. I glared at her coldly.

Miss Akard looked at me and then at the food.

"Excuse me. Am I intruding?" she looked curiously at me.

I simply stared at her in silence, hoping she would go away. I only wanted to talk to my mother and honor her on the anniversary of her death. Couldn't this woman understand that? She was ruining our special party. I wanted to be alone. Why was she here and sitting in my mother's seat on this day of all days? My eyes filled with tears, and I began to weep.

Miss Akard's expression suddenly changed, flooded with compassion and kindness. Her heart went out to me.

"Oh, poor child. I'm so sorry. I didn't mean to upset you. Please, don't cry," she wrapped her arms around me tenderly, catching her breath in alarm at the feel of my bones just beneath my skin.

The warmth of her hug surprised me. I had not been hugged for so long, not since my mother had died three years ago. I began crying aloud.

I suddenly found myself opening up my heart to her, telling her my story and pouring out my pent-up feelings of grief and loss. Her kind, tender eyes warmed and encouraged me. She wore gold-framed glasses similar to my mother's. For a moment, I saw the gentle kindness and light in her eyes that I had seen in my mother's. I instinctively trusted her, and I told her about my mother. I told her everything: the war, the soldier who saved my life, our move to Hanaokayama, my lessons, her sudden departure, and my daily picnics here as I waited for her to return for three years.

She listened patiently and compassionately for a long time. She didn't interrupt and let me speak candidly. Miss Akard nodded to show she was listening and seemed to take a genuine interest in my story.

"My mother was extremely positive and kind," I told her. "She encouraged me and helped me to be confident. She was able to find a reason to be happy about anything and always cheered me up by showing me the bright side of things. She was understanding and compassionate and always helped others before herself. She said that life is something that you should treasure and you should make the most of every day."

"Your mother sounds like a wonderful and courageous woman," she replied.

"She was the very best and kindest person. I admire, respect, and love her and think that she is truly the greatest mother in the entire world," I told her. I was so glad she understood how special my mother was.

"I don't want to interrupt your lunch, but I would love to learn more about your mother," she said. "Perhaps tomorrow at lunchtime I will see you here again?"

I smiled and bowed, "*Arigato gozaimasu,* thank you, Miss Akard. See you tomorrow."

Soon it became our regular custom to picnic together upon the hill and talk about my mother. I felt comfortable talking to Miss Akard. Her eyes were full of genuine concern and kindness, and she had a very gentle voice and refined manners that reminded me of my mother. She listened patiently and with great interest to everything I told her about my mother. It was wonderful to be able to speak to someone else about her, to share what she had taught me and to show her my notebook and the letter my mother had written to me.

I felt certain that my mother had sent Miss Akard to be my friend and to give me newfound hope in my dark and silent world. It was like the sunlight breaking upon the dark shadows of the valley below Hanaokayama. My perspective had suddenly transformed. Speaking about my mother somehow brought her spirit to life again. It was wonderful to share my memories and stories with someone who was interested in hearing about them and appreciated what an extraordinary person she was.

Miss Akard explained that she was originally from America and moved to Japan as a Christian missionary. She told me more about her school and suggested that I should consider taking the entrance exam to join the school. She said that I would meet lots of other kind and intelligent girls at the school who could be my friends.

"I think it's lovely that you have lunch with your mother here," she said, "but it would do you good to have friends your age, too. You can learn about history, art, drama, and music."

This made me think of my mother, too, and her education in Nagasaki. I wanted to learn what she had learned. She had always encouraged me to pursue my studies so that I could go on adventures and travel as she had not been able to do.

"I think I would like that very much," I said. "My mother showed me her school in Nagasaki. It sounds similar to your school. She studied so many subjects: history, art, music."

"That's wonderful," she replied. "I will speak to your brother about it and recommend that you register for the entrance exam."

"*Arigato gozaimasu*, thank you, Miss Akard," I bowed deeply with gratitude.

Miss Akard arranged a meeting with my brother to discuss the possibility of my joining the school. In the absence of my parents, he was now my guardian. He knew of the school's strong academic reputation and agreed that it would be a sensible plan for me to pursue my education there if I could qualify by passing the entrance exam.

"It's what our mother would have wanted," he said to me after meeting with Miss Akard. "Although, Mi-chan, be prepared for a very difficult exam."

Once I had received my brother's permission, I began to prepare for the rigorous entrance exam. There were several books that Miss Akard and my brother gave me to read. I would often take the books with me to Hanaokayama and read them while sitting on my favorite rock. I knew my mother was watching me study and could see that I took to heart her advice to focus on pursuing my studies and dreams. I knew she would approve of my studies and learning about the world to prepare me for my future adventures.

In the spring when the cherry blossoms were beginning to bloom, I took the exam. I was so nervous, but I remembered the lessons my mother had taught me. I remained calm and focused. I woke up early that day to see the sunrise and meditate. I could hear my mother's words, *Clear your mind*! I let my fear and anxiety flow away like water.

On the day the exam results were announced, I went to the school to discover my fate. The results were posted on the school grounds. Anxiously, I searched through the pages and found, to my surprise and jubilation, my name written in large, graceful characters. I had passed.

I was indescribably proud of my accomplishment and filled with pure joy for the first time since my mother's death. I knew my mother could see the writing, too, and what I had achieved. This was all thanks to her lessons and the wisdom she had passed down to me, which enabled me to be strong and have courage even in the darkest of times. I had been able to focus to achieve my dreams.

Even my brother said he was impressed with my results and pleased that I had been selected to join such a prestigious school.

"Mi-chan, you are finally growing up. Mother would be so proud," he said.

On my first day, I was very nervous as I put on my brand-new school uniform early in the morning. It was a long navy dress with long sleeves and a sailor collar, and I had new, matching navy shoes and a brown satchel for my notebooks and school books. I had spent so much time alone grieving on Hanaokayama and had distanced myself from the other children in my old school, running away immediately after lessons every day. The thought of a classroom full of girls was frightening. Then I remembered my promise to my mother. I would be strong and cheerful.

Freedom from fear gives you wings to soar. I remembered her wise words and smiled bravely as I walked into the hall of our grand and imposing school building for my induction. I felt she was watching over me and protecting me, and suddenly I felt much taller and more confident.

"*Ohayo gozaimasu*, good morning and welcome," Miss Akard greeted me warmly. It was reassuring to see a familiar face. She was wearing a starched white blouse and navy suit.

"Good morning, Miss Akard," I said. "I'm looking forward to my first day of school."

"There is someone I would like you to meet," she said. She motioned to a tall, slim, and pretty girl beside her with long hair and smiled. "This is Riko-san. This is her first day, too, and she is in your class."

The girl smiled and bowed. Her eyes beamed with mirth. She had a friendly demeanor and a kind expression.

"Thank you, Miss Akard. It's a pleasure to meet you, Riko-san. I'm Mimi," I said, and bowed.

"You're welcome. Why don't you ladies get acquainted? Riko-san, you can show her where the assembly hall is. We will have a welcome speech at 8:30," Miss Akard replied.

"*Arigato gozaimasu*, Miss Akard," I replied and bowed.

At first, I looked awkwardly at Riko and smiled nervously. I had spent so much time alone. I wasn't used to conversing with people my age. What would we talk about?

"Mimi, are you excited about school? There are so many people you should meet," she said excitedly. "You should have some breakfast, too. The food is delicious!"

"Thank you, Riko-san," I replied with relief. Her confidence and bubbliness instantly put me at ease. "That sounds great. I was feeling nervous this morning, but everyone is so welcoming, I feel much better now."

"I think everyone feels exactly the same," she said. "It's always the way on your first day at a new school! Come and meet everyone."

Instantly, I felt more relaxed and followed Riko. She took me to the hall, where all the pupils were having food and there was an energetic buzz of conversation and laughter. She went up to a circle of girls and they all greeted her enthusiastically. I looked at them curiously. I had spent so much time wondering what my new classmates would be like. They were all wearing their new uniforms like me and had smiling, fresh, fair faces and gentle manners. They spoke softly in impeccable Japanese and had the graceful, cultivated manners of young women who had been sheltered and privileged.

I remembered my brother's words that these girls were from some of the finest families in Kumamoto whose fortunes had survived even the war and whose fathers were now part of reshaping the future of Japanese business and industry. He explained that we shared a similar background, but that our lives had changed after our father's death and we lost our fortune. However, our mother was a fine lady from Nagasaki.

She trained us well and hoped we would have an excellent education. He reassured me that the school knew about our circumstances, but it wasn't necessary to draw attention to them. We should not dwell upon our suffering.

"Riko-san, there you are! We were wondering where you went. We assumed you went to get more food," one of the girls said.

"Yuki-san, Akiko-san, Mio-san, Etsuko-san, Hana-san, there is someone I'd like you to meet. This is Mimi-san," Riko said.

The girls all greeted me warmly and bowed.

"It's great to meet you, Mimi-san," Yuki said. "Isn't this a wonderful welcome? I've been so nervous about today that I thought I would faint, but everyone is so lovely."

"I felt exactly the same way!" I replied, laughing. "Miss Akard is so kind. She just introduced me to Riko-san."

"I have heard that Miss Akard is an excellent headmistress but can be very stern," Etsuko said.

"You're such a gossip, Etsuko-san," Riko chided her laughingly. "You just have to behave like a lady and you won't get into trouble."

"Miss Akard certainly introduced you to the right person. Riko-san knows everyone! She went to primary school with many of the girls who are here now," Akiko said.

"I'm so grateful to Miss Akard. She has been so kind to me," I said.

"Mimi-san, do you like music?" Hana asked me.

"Yes, I love to sing," I said. "My mother and I used to sing songs all the time."

"Well, then, we'll have lots in common, I love singing, and I play the koto, too," Hana replied.

"That's so impressive," I said. "I'd love to hear you play the koto. It's such an amazing instrument, and I think it sounds incredible."

"My mother said that we would learn how to cook, as well," Mio said.

"I'm terrible at cooking! She hopes I will learn to be an accomplished lady who can sing, paint, cook, and discuss history and that I will make a brilliant wife someday."

"She has high hopes for you," Etsuko said. "But if you can't cook, you won't be able to keep a house."

"Don't worry, Mio-san," I replied reassuringly. "I've recently learned how to cook and it's really fun. If I can learn how, anyone can!" We all laughed and talked about our favorite types of food.

Suddenly, I was no longer nervous and fearful but was excitedly talking with my new classmates about our hobbies, which subjects we were taking, and how much we had heard about the school from our families.

Soon I met lots of other girls in my class, and I quickly made friends. Miss Akard was right. They were all very friendly, welcoming, and honest, and the school had a strong sense of community. Over time, that initial circle of girls became my group of close and loyal friends. I was no longer isolated and grieving. Riko became my best friend, and I grew in confidence from her example, finally coming out of my place in the shadows after so long. All the girls called me "Mi-chan" now. I didn't tell them about my suffering and loneliness in the past since I had promised my brother that I would look ahead and not dwell on the past. They all came from very privileged backgrounds with stable families. I thought perhaps they would not understand, either. They didn't know what it was like to be an orphan.

I loved all of my lessons, especially history and art. We would learn sumi-e and watercolor painting outdoors in the garden on warm days. There were strawberry plants that climbed up the edge of one of the school fences from the field adjacent to our school. They tantalized us with their fruit glistening in the sunshine.

"Mi-chan," Riko said. "Look at these ripe strawberries! They look like sparkling rubies."

We were sitting at round tables in the garden with our paint boxes, brushes, and our cups filled with fresh water to clean our brushes.

"Oh, they look so delicious!" Hana said. "I wish I could eat just one."

"Why don't you ask if we can eat them?" Etsuko said.

"Oh, I couldn't," Hana replied.

"I will ask for permission," I said. I bravely went to the fence to speak to the farmer who was working on the adjacent field. He face was very tan from working in the sun, and he had deep lines around his forehead and eyes. He seemed surprised when he saw me walking towards him.

"*Konnichiwa*, good afternoon," I said to him and bowed. "We have been admiring your beautiful strawberries. You must be a very skilled farmer. We notice them every time we are outdoors for our art lesson. They would be a perfect subject to paint."

The man smiled with sincere gratitude. He bowed deeply with respect and said, "*Arigato gozaimasu*, thank you for your kind words. I would be honored to share them with you and your friends so you could paint them. I see you have water cups, so you could wash them and eat them afterwards."

He picked us strawberries and gave them to me over the fence. I bowed and replied, "*Arigato gozaimasu*, thank you so much! We appreciate your generosity in sharing these with us. We will paint them and enjoy them and always remember your kindness."

"*Arigato gozaimasu*," my friends echoed and bowed from a distance.

I returned to my friends and triumphantly gave each of them a strawberry.

"*Domo arigato*, thank you!" Hana said.

"You are so kind, Mi-chan," Etsuko said.

"You're so brave, Mi-chan!" Mio laughed.

"I knew I liked you when I met you," Riko said. "You are fearless, Mi-chan!"

"Thanks, Riko-chan. I learned that from my mother. We must show *kansha* for these ripe strawberries and the farmer who has grown them," I said.

We painted birds and flowers in black sumi-e and delicate water-colors, and I perfected my brushstrokes for bamboo leaves and stalks. I covered scrolls of rice paper with the same uniform strokes until it became second nature to me. My art teacher said I was making great progress, and I was proud to show my brother my paintings.

"You are learning to be very disciplined and applying yourself to your studies, Mi-chan. I have heard very positive reports from your headmistress and your teachers. Mother would be very happy," he said and nodded approvingly.

I beamed. I felt certain she would be proud of me, too.

I found that I didn't have my mother's gift of singing, although I still loved to sing and sang with my friends, including Hana, who was a very talented musician. Her voice and her koto playing were stunning. She even played "Sakura" on the koto for me. The lilting, melancholy sound of the koto reminded me so much of my mother that tears came to my eyes.

I enjoyed learning about music theory, history, and famous compos-ers. Although I couldn't play an instrument, I found great pleasure in listening to talented musicians perform and could appreciate the vari-ous stylings of renowned composers and the history behind their work.

I discovered I had a flair for creative storytelling. When my friends were struggling to write, I would tell them stories to inspire them, just as my mother had.

"If only I could tell stories like you, Mi-chan!" Akiko said.

"If only I could play badminton and run like you!" I replied. We both laughed.

"Isn't it amazing that we all have different talents? I am a musician, Akiko is an athlete, Riko is a chef, Yuki is a dancer, Mio is a poet, Etsuko is a painter, and you are a storyteller, Mi-chan," Hana said.

My passion for acting was a surprise discovery. I started by reading monologues from plays dramatically in class, and everyone praised my reading. Then one of my teachers told me that I should audition for a school play. I was nervous, as I had never acted before, but I remembered my promise to my mother. Riko encouraged me and said I had a natural flair for the dramatic, and she helped me rehearse my monologue from Shakespeare's *Romeo and Juliet* for the audition.

"I'm so scared, Riko-chan. I'm going to cancel the audition. I can't do it!" I said one day as we were rehearsing. The thought of the audience suddenly terrified me, and my hands were trembling.

"No fear, remember, Mi-chan? You taught me that. You will be superb. Just believe in yourself and be yourself on stage," she said. I felt that she echoed my mother's sentiments exactly, and this reminded me to be strong. I remembered my mother's words, and I could hear her voice. *What's the worst that could happen? Be strong and free, Mi-chan.*

"Thank you, Riko-chan," I said. "You're right. No fear!"

After that first step into the unknown on stage, I began to act and excelled at it so much that I was cast as the lead in several school plays. One of my teachers also introduced me to a local radio station so I could help with a children's radio show after school. I found that I loved transforming into new characters, performing on stage in front of an audience, and speaking on the radio. It was exciting and gave me an exhilarating sense of confidence and power. It reminded me of the times my mother and I sang together on Hanaokayama. I felt completely free and fearless, like I was a sparrow flying above the mountain. I could share the power of emotion and the beauty of language with hundreds of others and inspire them. I could be anyone, assume any character, and be transported into a magical world, just like on Hanaokayama. It just took a shift of perspective, and I could become one with any character and see the world through different eyes.

When I stood on stage in the spotlight, I felt that my mother could see me, that she was watching with the rest of the audience and could hear the thunderous applause. I felt proud that she could see me being truly strong and happy as I had promised her. I secretly dedicated every single performance to her memory.

"Bravo, Mi-chan!" Riko, Hana, Akiko, Yuki, Mio, and Etsuko greeted me after the curtain fell on the final act. Their fresh faces were beaming with joy, and their arms were filled with colorful bouquets of flowers tied with ribbon for me.

"I'm so proud of you, Mi-chan. I knew you'd be incredible!" Riko said.

"You were brilliant. Even I get nervous when I play the koto in front of such a large crowd, but you were so confident," Hana said.

"I agree, there's so much pressure but you were a pro, Mi-chan," Yuki said.

"If it were a competition, you would be the winner," Akiko said.

Even Etsuko, who was usually critical, admitted, "You were the best by far, Mi-chan. There was nothing to find fault with."

"You brought Shakespeare's poetic words to life, Mi-chan," Mio said approvingly.

"Thank you so much! I'm so grateful for all your support and for such dear friends," I said, overcome with emotion at this outpouring of love and kindness.

Then I heard steps behind us. I turned and saw my brother

approaching. His stern face transformed into a smile as he saw me gathered with my friends.

"Mi-chan, congratulations," he said, and bowed. "It was an excellent performance."

"Thank you," I bowed.

Finally, I was truly happy and strong as I had promised my mother I would be. I was no longer pretending. It was genuine.

Look at the world in a new way and
you will discover *kibo*, hope.

CHAPTER 11

MIKATA / PERSPECTIVE

"Today, December 18, 1956, is a historic day. Japan has become a member of the United Nations," explained Miss Akard, dressed in her usual crisp white blouse and navy blue suit during our history lecture. "Therefore, today's lesson will examine the purpose of the United Nations."

I sat at the front of the classroom, trying to comprehend the rudiments of international relations. I diligently took notes in my notebook. At the end of the lecture, I gathered my books and notes and put them in my satchel.

"I have a special book for you." Miss Akard smiled as she handed me a large volume entitled *Thomas Jefferson*.

"*Arigato gozaimasu*, thank you, Miss Akard," I said excitedly and accepted the gift eagerly. "He wrote the Declaration of Independence," I said, my eyes shining. I bowed many times with gratitude.

"We hold these truths to be self-evident, that all men are created equal, that they are endowed by their Creator with certain unalienable rights, that among these are life, liberty, and the pursuit of happiness," I quoted proudly.

"That's very impressive," she said, smiling. "I think you will enjoy the book. You deserve it. You have done so well in your history lessons, and it has been a privilege teaching you and watching your progress over the years. I can't believe this is your final year."

"Thank you so much. I will treasure this always," I said.

"Thomas Jefferson once said, 'I like the dreams of the future better than the history of the past.' History is very important, but never forget that your dreams are, too. The world is yours to discover, and your life is an adventure that is yet to be written," she said.

"Thank you, Miss Akard. I won't forget," I said.

Miss Akard had gone to great lengths to teach and inspire me. The school community she fostered under her leadership was a positive and inclusive one that valued kindness, integrity, and the pursuit of knowledge. She had opened my mind with her teachings of American history, and I learned so much about the world, history, politics, and other cultures. Like my mother, she taught me to open my mind to new possibilities and ways of thinking. She helped me to understand my mother's love and courage in teaching me and caring for me despite her own illness and suffering. From Miss Akard, I learned that my mother had given me an extraordinary gift that would remain with me forever.

Miss Akard was a truly inspirational teacher and headmistress who rekindled my love of adventure and my dream of exploring the world, and to this day, I am grateful to her. I had a thirst for knowledge and eagerly absorbed all of the books, lectures, and lessons I had the privilege of encountering at school. They revealed new horizons for me.

Suddenly the world was as vast a universe as my mind, and I had so many new ideas to assimilate. My appreciation for, and wonder at, the world grew as my mind and knowledge expanded.

Miss Akard also encouraged me to volunteer at a local orphanage after school to help care for young children who had lost their parents during the war. Through helping others, I forgot my own sadness, and, as my mother had taught me, I gained a greater sense of perspective and compassion.

My mother's eternal love and my dream of seeing the world gave me strength to look toward a bright and adventurous future that now seemed so tangible and full of promise. The world was no longer such a vague and nebulous concept and not simply an ocean with tall ships and an unknown beyond. I could see our world much more clearly, now with greater understanding of different cultures, geographies, and histories. I was eager to explore the places I had read about, especially America, which fascinated me. I admired the ideals of democracy and equality upon which the country was founded and the right of all citizens to the pursuit of happiness. This reminded me of my promise to my mother.

"You will see the world someday," Miss Akard said.

"My mother said I would," I replied. "It's in my genes since my mother is from Nagasaki, which was Japan's gateway to the world."

"Yes, you are fortunate," she replied. "You have been given a global perspective and such a tremendous imagination. The sky is the limit."

Through the introduction of Miss Akard, my studies, and my close and supportive friends, Hanaokayama had renewed me again with hope. The dazzling light of the rising sun over the mountain had obliterated the darkness of fear and despair in the valley below.

When, after many happy and fulfilling years as a pupil, my last day of school drew to a close, I bid a tearful farewell to my close circle of friends and my headmistress Miss Akard, who was retiring from a long and illustrious career in education. It was emotional to part with such fond friends and memories and a place that had inspired me intellectually and provided a heartwarming sense of community and belonging after being isolated for so long. However, I knew that my exciting and unconventional journey would continue beyond this chapter.

I also said a silent farewell to my career on the stage, and I shed a tear as the curtain closed on my last performance. Although others had suggested that I study drama at college, and I had been tempted by the idea, I decided not to pursue a career in acting. I would certainly miss the performances and the roar of the crowd. Like my mother's boundless love, that magical experience of transformation and the confidence it gave me would stay with me forever.

"Remember—no fear, Mi-chan, and we will always be best friends," Riko said as she embraced me on our last day of school.

"I promise, Riko-chan," I said. "You, too. Thank you so much for everything."

"I can't believe it's ended," Hana said sadly.

"I remember I was so scared on the first day. My mother was right when she said not to worry since it would soon be over. The time has gone so quickly," Yuki said wistfully.

"It's been so fun, I will miss you all!" Akiko sighed.

"Hasn't it been an exciting adventure? Now we'll have to get adjusted to ordinary life. My mother says I need to think about settling down and getting married," Mio said. "At least I can cook now! But it won't be the same without seeing all of you together every day."

"Ladies, this is the end of my teaching career. It has been such a pleasure and privilege to teach all of you. Remember that this is only the beginning of your own adventures," Miss Akard said to us with her warm and understanding smile. "Hold this love and friendship in your heart wherever you go, and never let go of your dreams. Remember our school motto: 'gratitude and service.' You will all lead extraordinary lives and serve and guide others with courage, compassion, and appreciation. I am proud of all of you."

"Thank you, Miss Akard, and thank you, Mi-chan, Riko-chan, Yuki-chan, Akiko-chan, Hana-chan, and Mio-chan," Etsuko said, visibly moved and suddenly more solemn than ever before. "I've loved every minute here and I will miss it so much, but we will always have our memories and our friendship."

At this emotional and heartfelt declaration, the tears flowed freely down my cheeks. I said, "*Domo arigato*, thank you so much to you all. This has been one of the best experiences of my life. I will always treasure your love and friendship. I wish you all the very best for your future adventures."

We all embraced each other again. We vowed to keep in touch and remain lifelong friends, never letting distance separate us. They were all planning to stay in Kumamoto and build their lives there, even Hana, although she had been offered a place at a music conservatory in Tokyo. I was the only one who was forging an independent path to the unknown, but this was hardly surprising since I had already led a very different life than the rest of them. They all had deep roots in the community and valued stability and proximity to family, but I was free and had the adventurer's wandering spirit.

True to their initial promises, my loyal circle of friends did stay in Kumamoto and remained close to their families. They all eventually married men from Kumamoto and went on to raise their own families. Years later, I would learn that some of them even sent their daughters to our school, which was a testament to how much this wonderful place had inspired us with its Christian ethos of compassion and service.

At eighteen years old, I was no longer a frail and fearful child, but a confident and self-assured woman with bright, inquisitive dark eyes, a slim figure, and short, stylish hair. Since I had graduated, I no longer wore my usual navy uniform and brown satchel. I finally had proper grown-up clothing, which made me look more mature, sophisticated, and stylish. When I looked in the mirror, I could barely recognize myself and was struck by the transformation. I was rosy-cheeked, healthy, and filled with joy. Happiness emanated from my very being like sunlight, and it seemed to illuminate my large, dark eyes and tan complexion with an ethereal, confident glow. There was no trace of fear. I had made a decision that was set to change the course of my life.

I had to make a final visit to Hanaokayama to tell my mother the momentous news. I wore a new dress in her honor. It was a long, blue cotton dress with short sleeves, a defined waist, and a full skirt in the latest fashion.

I vividly remember walking up that venerable hillside for the very last time before leaving Kumamoto. I walked slowly so that I could soak up every detailed memory and capture every precious moment in my mind to revisit in the future. My long dress fluttered in the breeze. I gazed admiringly at the singing birds, blossoming flowers, and strong, majestic trees, as though I were seeing them for the first time, like the day I had learned about clearing my mind and existing fully in the present moment. Everywhere, I saw life. Everywhere, I saw my mother. But, somehow, this time I felt better and more serene than I had ever felt before. The pool in my mind was as clear as crystal again, unsullied by regret, anger, and fear.

"Oka-chan, I know you are still with me. I waited here for you to return, and it took me a very long time to realize that you had never really left. You are everywhere," I said as I gazed down at the valley below, admiring the new green leaves on the trees. I observed the new buildings in the city that had replaced those devastated in the war.

So much had changed since the war, and the city had gradually blossomed like a flower in the nurturing sun and refreshing morning rain. Truly the people of Kumamoto, like our countrymen across Japan, had banded together to rebuild our community from dust and despair. Their unbreakable spirit of courage and hope had repaired the devastation and made our city whole and glittering again like a phoenix rising from the ashes. The new buildings existed alongside the ancient, and the landscape had changed to accommodate our ever-living history and to reflect the evolution of our city and our country after the war.

"Mother, I want to thank you for your love and for making me promise to live. It has saved me and given me hope during the darkest times," I said. "And you have sent me so many kind and supportive friends. Thank you."

I thought of the endless days and hours I had sat alone on this mountain during my solitary picnics and cried until I thought I had no tears left to cry. Those days of darkness and isolation were now behind me, and I thought gratefully of Miss Akard and all of my school friends, who had brought so much love, support, and inspiration into my life.

"I promise that I will always be happy and strong. I will live a full life for you and the soldier who gave his life for me. I will dream and challenge life fearlessly, like you. As you once told me, freedom from fear gives us wings to soar," I said.

I stretched and raised my hands to the sky as if to touch the sun. The sparrows were flying overhead. Soon I would be traveling, like them, across the ocean to a new land I had never seen before in my life. I thought of the ships leaving the harbor in Nagasaki in a dazzling sea of light. My mother said I would see the world, and now this prophecy had come true.

I looked to the pristine and cloudless sky where the stars would be at night, and finally I saw her face clearly before me, glancing down over me with a familiar, understanding, and gentle smile. I felt she was present in the trees, in the swaying grass, and the silken petals of the wildflowers. She was everywhere, just like kami, the sacred essence that flowed through all of nature, connecting all life with a deep and eternal spirit. It had taken me years to grasp this, but I finally understood. She had not really left me behind, even in her death. She was ever present and watching over me, like the ageless face of Hanaokayama, and only now did I have the maturity and wisdom to realize this. This is what she meant when she said in my letter that I would see her if I looked to the stars. She would always be with me no matter where life would take me.

"Oka-chan, I am going to college in America," I said. I paused and reflected upon how important and life-changing of a decision this was: a new country and higher education to prepare me for a career. I had strayed far from the traditional journey of a young woman from Kumamoto. Instead of marrying a local man from a respectable family and becoming a dutiful housewife, I was forging an independent path of my own, inspired by my mother, my education, and the fearlessness she had taught me.

"You were right," I said. "You said I would see the world and be adventurous. Even though I am leaving Japan, I will always carry your spirit of love and courage in my heart, and I will see you when I look at the stars. Thank you for teaching me that even in darkness, love's brilliance will illuminate your path. I will never forget this magical place and the lessons of courage, perspective, and self-reliance I have learned. I shall cherish the memory of Hanaokayama forever. It will always live in my heart, and I will see the beauty of this place and its wisdom wherever I go."

I knew that no matter where I traveled, I could revisit Hanaokayama in my mind, just as my mother had promised. To this day, it remains stored in a special drawer in my mind, and I can return to my favorite spot on the rock at any time.

I heard the soothing chanting of the monks in the distance, and I remembered the first day that we had arrived at the mountain and had met the kind priest who knew my mother. It was very similar to this day—one full of the hope and beauty of spring, of new life and promise. Now I understood why we had come to live there and what the mountain had truly taught us. I was not alone in this recognition of the mountain's power and serenity. The temple which was being built when I lived on Hanaokayama was dedicated to world peace and honored the memory of those who died during World War II. It was built by hand by Nichidatsu Fujii and his monks, and was the first of many Buddhist peace pagodas he and his followers built around the world. To this day, visitors come to enjoy the magnificent view, timeless beauty, and tranquility of this place.

These priceless gifts I received from Hanaokayama would remain with me forever, and I promised then and there that I would pass them down to my children and to others someday. I vowed that I would honor my mother by sharing her story of undying love and courage with the world. I knew this wisdom must be shared, for it could help thousands of others like me. Although it has taken me seventy-two years to share it, and I am now eighty-one years old, I am proud to be fulfilling my promise to my mother at last. This is her legacy, which I am now humbly passing on to future generations in her honor. Her spirit of love and courage will live forever and continue to inspire others and illuminate their paths as they have inspired me and illuminated mine.

"*Arigato*, thank you, Oka-chan." I bowed very low to her with the deepest respect, so low that my hair and forehead touched the tall grass. I would have bowed even lower if I could. My gratitude and respect for her are endless.

Then I turned to survey Hanaokayama, this enchanted mountain. I didn't know then how long I would be away from Kumamoto and that I would never live in Japan again, but somehow I sensed it. There was a significant feeling of finality to this farewell. It was both a joyful and bittersweet occasion, and I could see this very moment passing before my eyes and disappearing like the blossoms scattered by the breeze, as fleeting and evanescent as my mother had taught me life would always be. I was leaving home at last, and I needed to say good-bye properly to this place that had been my refuge and my inspiration for so many years.

I bowed to the temple and the sacred torii. I thought of the broken yet defiant torii in Nagasaki and the spirit of faith and courage that could never be destroyed, just like my mother's spirit.

I shouted to the great trees, our little house, the well, the soaring birds, and my colorful wildflower friends, "*Arigato, arigato*, thank you, thank you from the bottom of my heart! I will always remember you." My cheerful voice rang through the mountain, and I felt they understood my kansha, my appreciation, for their friendship.

I slowly wandered down the familiar hillside path for the last time before my journey to America, with the magnificent trees saluting me as I passed with light steps as though I were floating in a dream. The creamy cherry blossoms were falling like fresh snow and covered my ebony hair, a reminder of the old soldier's gift of courage and his valiant act of sacrifice that had saved my life. I thought of mono no aware, the impermanence of life, but then I also reflected that, despite this, some things remained forever and could never be destroyed, not even by death or the passage of time.

The sweet fragrance of flowers filled the fresh spring air, and there were magnificent clouds of blossoms before me like a painting. Suddenly, I could hear the sound of my mother's silvery voice singing "Sakura."

Cherry blossoms, cherry blossoms, floating in the spring sky, as far as you can see. Is it a mist or clouds? The air is fragrant. Let's see the blossoms at last.

I looked up at the dancing blossoms as they pirouetted in the sky, observing that perfect and ephemeral moment before they fell to the ground forever. I captured that moment in my heart and danced with them in appreciation of their eternal beauty, grace, and strength of spirit, which, like my mother's spirit, love, and courage, would always inspire and never fade.

Mikata, perspective, is the key to happiness
in life. It can transform everything.

Masuko, Mimi's mother

Mimi at school

Kyushu Jogakuin, Mimi's school

ABOUT THE AUTHOR AND THE INSPIRATION FOR THIS STORY

Mia Iwama Hastings

Mia Iwama Hastings is the author of *The Height of Fearlessness*, which is based on true events from her mother's early life in Japan. Born and raised in California, Mia graduated magna cum laude from Brown University with a BA in Classics and holds an MA in English from University College London. Mia is a marketing specialist. She lives in London with her husband Richard.

Mimi Iwama

Mimi Iwama's early life inspired *The Height of Fearlessness*. She was born in Kumamoto, Japan. She moved to the United States in 1959 to study at the School of International Service at American University in Washington, D.C. She has worked for local newspaper, radio and television outlets and in community development and public relations in California. She has four children.

Mimi decided to collaborate with her youngest daughter, Mia, to fulfill her lifelong dream of sharing her mother's inspirational story and wisdom with the world.